# The Road to Success
# How to Manage Growth

The Grant Thornton LLP Guide for Entrepreneurs

# The Road to Success

## How to Manage Growth

Mendy Kwestel
Michael Preston
Gary Plaster

John Wiley & Sons, Inc.

New York • Chichester • Weinheim • Brisbane • Singapore • Toronto

Appendix A Copyright © 1996 by Peter M. Panken. All rights reserved.

Appendix B from *AUDITING*, Third Edition, by Dan M. Guy, C. Wayne Alderman, and Alan J. Winters, copyright © 1993 by Harcourt Brace & Company, reproduced by permission of the publisher.

Appendix C reprinted by permission of *FORBES ASAP Magazine* © Forbes Inc., 1997.

This text is printed on acid-free paper.

This publication is designed to provide accurate and authoritative information in regard to the subject matter covered. It is sold with the understanding that the publisher is not engaged in rendering legal, accounting, or other professional services. If legal advice or other expert assistance is required, the services of a competent professional person should be sought.

*Library of Congress Cataloging in Publication Data:*
Kwestel, Mendy.
    The Grant Thornton LLP guide for entrepreneurs : the road to success : how to manage growth / Mendy Kwestel, Michael Preston, Gary Plaster.
        p.    cm.
    Includes index.
    ISBN 0-471-17245-6 (cloth)
    1. Strategic planning.  2. Industrial management.  3. Success in business.  4. Entrepreneurship.  I. Preston, Michael, 1942–   .
II. Plaster, Gary.  III. Title.
HD30.28.K93   1997
658.4′012—dc21                                                97-20736
                                                                    CIP

Printed in the United States of America

10   9   8   7   6   5   4   3   2   1

# Contents

# CONTENTS

# Preface

We've seen it again and again: an entrepreneur has a great idea for a company; the management team works really hard and the company grows by leaps and bounds, until suddenly . . . it hits a wall.

Take Charles Travis, the founder of Travis Housewares. When we met him, he had 14 factories in as many cities, hundreds of employees, $80 million a year in revenues—but he was still personally opening all the company mail. He was putting in 18-hour days, and so was his loyal but small staff, but his midsized company was stalled out. It couldn't get any bigger because he, personally, couldn't work any harder, and he didn't have the team or the infrastructure to expand. Charles Travis had hit the wall.

We at Grant Thornton have made a name for ourselves by advising midsized owner-managed entrepreneurial companies on how to get past that wall. The solutions are not always the same. Each new client who walks through our doors has a completely fascinating story of a good idea, good timing, hard work triumphing over adversity, luck, the thrill of victory, and the agony of the corporate tax code. Each of their stories is unique, of course, but over the years what we've been struck by are the similarities of the problems they face.

How do you take a mom-and-pop company and turn it into a corporate giant? How do you develop the information systems and the long-range planning processes that make this possible? How do you put together a team of skilled managers, and then how do you give up enough control to let them do their jobs? And after you've done all that, how do you keep your finger on the pulse of a now quickly expanding company?

Unfortunately, when entrepreneurs turn to the business book-shelves for answers to these questions, they find trendy one-word mantras like "re-engineering" or "downsizing," or complicated 25-part, multi-year plans full of business jargon.

Now don't get us wrong. We *like* business jargon. But our clients are not accountants or consultants, generally not MBAs, and certainly not interested in the fine differences between a regulation D equity offering and a regulation A equity offering, except as it affects their own situation. They want plainspoken, practical advice.

And that advice just can't be one-size-fits-all. General business books may make points that are *applicable* to a stalled-out midsized business, but they don't address the specific problems we run across every day. We know, because we've read them.

Hence, this book. We're going to show you how to avoid the common pitfalls of growing a company, how to build a team, implement a business plan, establish good information reporting, and make use of the new information systems and controls. We will also address the critical issues of finding and retaining top-notch people, forming a board of directors, and—one of the more overlooked problems of entrepreneurial companies—how to plan for succession to ensure the survival of the company past the first generation.

*The Road to Success—How to Manage Growth* addresses those companies who have successfully raised capital and developed their product or concept, but who now face a new challenge: managing growth. Our intention was not to write a textbook, but rather to recount the true-life stories and hard-won experiences of entrepreneurs who have met that challenge.

We have changed the names of both individuals and companies, but we feel sure you will be able to tell that every drop of blood and sweat—and every cry of triumph—in these stories is real.

In chapter one, we will discuss common problems of growing entrepreneurial companies: how the paramount need to survive can eclipse the equally paramount need for infrastructure; how a management team can fail to keep pace with a company's growth; how an entrepreneur's need for control can sabotage his ability to lead; and how the lack of long-term planning and the ineffective implementation of technology can bring even a thriving company to its knees.

In chapter two, we discuss the first key element in coming to grips with these problems: the strategic plan. We detail a five-step process a management team can use to analyze its strengths and weaknesses, examine current and potential opportunities, and—with this information—develop a strategy for the future.

Chapter three describes how to reorganize a rapidly expanding entrepreneurial company. We outline several tried-and-true structural systems, but describe in some detail the one structure we have found most effective: organizing around a company's critical processes.

In today's business environment, no company can survive without timely information reporting. In chapter four we discuss how a rapidly expanding entrepreneurial company goes about developing an information reporting system that allows its management team to get the same "feel" for their company they used to get when the company was small enough for them to physically visit all the sites, look over inventory, and greet every employee by his or her first name.

In chapter five we examine the myriad issues related to information technology: how to measure its true cost and assess its effectiveness; how to undertake the sensible acquisition of information technology; how to implement that technology once it has been acquired; and how to integrate it into the day-to-day operations of the company.

Only 37% of entrepreneurial companies are successfully passed on to the next generation, a result of the general lack of planning for succession. In chapter six, we describe how an entrepreneur can successfully pass the torch and ensure the continued survival of his or her company—surely as integral a part of the infrastructure of a business as any of the other topics we've covered in this book.

In chapter seven we discuss finding and retaining good people—a process that presents special challenges for expanding entrepreneurial companies. Because of their rapid expansion, they are not only filling jobs, but creating positions that have never existed before.

In chapter eight, we make the case for an institution that many entrepreneurs resist at first: a board of directors. As most entrepreneurial companies who try it discover, the advantages of a board are astonishingly rich and varied, and we go into each of those advantages in detail.

For quick reference, at the end of each chapter we include Entrepreneur's Summaries. At the end of this book we include an appendix with some very specific information related to the legal aspects of employment.

If it was an entrepreneurial spirit that built this country, it is that same spirit that's fueling the engine for growth in the 1990s. In 1995, a record 770,000 businesses were incorporated. According to the National Federation of Independent Businesses, nearly 3.5 *million* U.S. small businesses were launched in 1995, many of them started by corporate managers who had been downsized during the preceding five years. Of these businesses, of course, only a small fraction will survive five years, and only a fraction of this fraction will ever pass the $10-million-a-year revenues mark.

The successes of those entrepreneurs who have risen to a level where they even have a *chance* to hit the wall are a testament to their enormous drive, ambition, and hard work. Paradoxically, it is often these same qualities that make it difficult for them to get beyond their current plateau.

The very attributes that made Charles Travis (and most larger-than-life entrepreneurs) so successful in the first place are the same attributes that are holding them back as they try to grow their companies.

The genius of an entrepreneur consists of risking everything on a great idea, launching it at the perfect moment, and then selling the product with a singleness of purpose that borders on obsession. Many times, the only thing that gets the product onto store shelves in the first place is the entrepreneur's own certainty. And the only thing that keeps it there is a trait that would seem to be in complete contradiction to the entrepreneur's single-mindedness—a flexibility that somehow allows entrepreneurs to relish living out on the edge. An entrepreneur almost has to enjoy risking everything on a single roll of the dice.

Now consider the traits necessary to run a rapidly expanding business: Yes, you have to make your product, market your product, and sell your product. And flexibility is at a premium. But then come all the things entrepreneurs find less exciting. You have to count your product, process orders, hire and manage people, bill and collect the money, deposit the money, invest the money. You have to collect information, analyze the information, disseminate information to investors, lenders, and regulators who then want to second-guess decisions that up until now have been yours to make alone.

All these things call for talents that are completely different from, and in some cases diametrically opposed to, the talents that got the entrepreneur this far in the first place.

But that is not to say that it can't be done. In this book you'll hear the stories of dozens of entrepreneurs and their companies as they struggle to keep control of their own rapid growth, impose infrastructure in the midst of chaos, and eventually emerge victorious.

# Acknowledgments

We would like to acknowledge the contribution of Peter M. Panken, Esq., a partner in the New York–based law firm of Parker Chapin Flattau & Klimpl, LLP, who wrote the section on "Establishing Effective Employment Practices" in Appendix A. His input on the legal ramifications of employee policies was invaluable.

There were many partners, managers, and staff members at Grant Thornton who reviewed the many drafts and gave us the benefit of their professional experiences and expertise. We are indebted to them all. In particular, we would like to thank the professionals in our strategic consulting group who provided us with information and guidance throughout the writing of the manuscript. Finally, we want to express our gratitude to Domenick J. Esposito, Northeast region managing partner of Grant Thornton LLP, who developed the concept of the *Grant Thornton LLP Guide for Entrepreneurs* and encouraged us to write this book.

# More Help for Entrepreneurs

*The Road to Success—How to Manage Growth,* part of the *Grant Thornton LLP Guide for Entrepreneurs,* is the second in a series of books designed to provide entrepreneurs with simple, practical advice on critical issues and challenges facing growing companies. The first book in the series, *Raising Capital: The Grant Thornton LLP Guide for Entrepreneurs,* is a practical how-to book and reference tool. *Raising Capital* discusses various capital market alternatives, including the process of going public, and evaluates the pros and cons of different options.

Also included as part of the series are:

- A growing number of informative guides geared towards entrepreneurial companies, including *Reinventing Financial Reporting* and *Trends in Corporate Governance*

- Periodic surveys of growing companies on critical financial and operational issues

- Seminars addressing issues and opportunities in capital markets, both domestically and globally

Grant Thornton LLP is the only CPA firm with partners serving on the Listing and Review Committee to the board of directors of NASDAQ and the hearing panel to this committee. They are well versed in issues surrounding NASDAQ listing requirements and corporate governance rules of publicly held companies.

In addition, Grant Thornton LLP sponsors the Best Practices Council of the National Association of Corporate Directors, as well as regional seminars conducted by the NACD for corporate directors throughout the country.

For more information about Grant Thornton LLP's services to entrepreneurs and growing companies, please contact:

Mr. Mendy Kwestel
Partner and Director of Entrepreneurial Services
Grant Thornton LLP
605 Third Avenue
New York, NY 10158

# The Problems of Growing Entrepreneurial Companies

In 1993, Larry Jones sat at a national trade organization banquet held in his honor. He had just been named "Entrepreneur of the Year" by his peers. The speaker at the dais described to the audience how Larry had formed a company called LJ Electronics only three years before to buy up the rights to under-performing consumer electronics products. Using creative marketing and attention-getting packaging, his company had gone from yearly revenues of less than $2 million in 1990 to $20 million by 1993. In that time, Larry had taken the company public, opened three new plants, bought several new product lines—and no one at the banquet knew it yet, but his investment bank was already exploring opportunities for additional financing in order to expand even further.

If anyone had gone up to Larry that night and told him that within the next year, his company would post a loss of $6 million and be on the brink of bankruptcy, he would have laughed at the impossibility of it—but in fact that's exactly what happened.

## INFRASTRUCTURE

Larry wasn't laughing when he came to see us. The stock price had plunged, and there were real doubts as to whether the company could survive. When clients like Larry come to us, our first objective is to identify the *immediate* cause of the problem. In this case, it was easy to spot: a severe underestimation of the effects of discounts and volume rebates. Sales were going up exponentially, but the deep discounts, charge-backs, and promotions that were becoming a norm in the industry meant that an item that listed for $20.00 was in some cases actually only bringing in $5.00. Somehow, in the process of the company's rapid growth, no one noticed they were selling the product for less than it cost to make.

But if runaway discounts were what brought Larry Jones and the LJ Electronics Company to their knees, the *underlying* cause of the collapse was much more fundamental: infrastructure.

They didn't have any.

We define infrastructure as the organizational framework, back-office support, and information systems necessary to provide management with the information and data it needs to run the ongoing day-to-day operations of a company and to make decisions about current and future strategies for the business. LJ Electronics' management was too busy making money to notice how little they really knew about their situation.

It's a weakness we see in many rapidly expanding small and medium-sized companies. Naturally, in the beginning, the focus of any start-up has to be on sales (no sales, no company) and on production (no product, no sales). As we said in the introduction, most new companies have limited capital, so it makes sense for them to spend it on the priority items. Slightly more forward-thinking new companies might also throw a few dollars at marketing and research and development. But few brand-new companies put a high priority on building an organization, putting a management team in place, and creating an information system. They're too busy staying alive.

We were listening to a young entrepreneur talk about this not long ago. She'd recently started an imaging company, and things were going very well. She had hired eight employees, and was looking to hire a few more to take care of rapidly increasing business. We asked about her tax planning, and she looked sheepish and said she'd been putting it off. In fact, she admitted, the company's taxes were due the very next day, and she was going to be pulling an all-nighter. She said, "I've been meaning to do some planning, but every day there's always something more important, a better use of my time. I'm so concerned about survival, about making a sale."

This is the entrepreneurial mentality, and really, you can't fault it. After all, it had gotten her this far. A large percentage of new companies fail in the first 12 months, but this woman's imaging business won't be one of them; her old-fashioned entrepreneurial hustle and drive are clearly working for her.

You could argue that if she doesn't have time to prepare the company's income tax returns, it would be wise for her to hire someone to do them for her. You could also argue that one of the most important things she could be doing right now would be to set up her business from a tax-wise standpoint in order to maximize the amount of money she and her company are earning.

In fact, we *did* make these arguments. But we didn't press the point, because (1) we could see our advice was falling on deaf ears; and (2) with gross revenues of under $5 million, her business can survive and even prosper right now without a lot of planning and infrastructure.


But what happens when it gets a little bigger? This was the situation Larry Jones and LJ Electronics were facing after about a year in business. Money was beginning to flow in, and LJ Electronics had to decide where to spend it. Larry wanted growth; his stockholders wanted growth; the industry wanted growth. So LJ Electronics put its money almost exclusively into revenue-producing areas: new products, new plants, new markets.

Naturally, a little money got spent along the way on back-office support. Larry hired a CFO and a few other key management people. But for a company growing as fast as LJ Electronics, the lack of infrastructure was pretty staggering. The light management team and the rudimentary information system that had been put in place were swamped by the expansion of overall company operations.

This meant that when small warning bells should have started going off, not only was no one listening—the warning bells weren't even hooked up to the house current.


What are the problems a company faces as it makes the transition from entrepreneurial start-up to rapidly expanding midsized company? Lots of books have been written about the problems from *without*—a changing marketplace, overseas competition, economic downturns—but this chapter is about the problems that come from *within:*

- The ineffective deployment of human resources

- The typical entrepreneur's hesitancy to delegate

- A lack of understanding of the importance of "people issues"

- The lack of long-term planning

- The ineffective implementation of technology

In our experience, these are the problems that can prevent any entrepreneurial company from achieving greatness. Ignoring these problems, particularly in today's marketplace, can lead to economic disaster. Let's begin with human resources.

## HUMAN RESOURCES: "WE HAVE NO MIDDLE MANAGEMENT"

Travis Housewares was an LJ Electronics waiting to happen. In two years they'd gone from gross sales of $30 million to $80 million, with no sign of any slowdown in expansion. The reason for their success? Sixty-year-old Charles Travis, the entrepreneur who'd started the company seven years before. This man could sell anything. His line of household items was so hot that the company had 10 plants all over the Midwest working overtime to meet demand.

But in January of 1995, Travis Housewares had no CFO, no information officer, and no chief operating officer. These positions had not suddenly become vacant; these positions had simply never existed.

"I recognize that we have no middle management," Travis told us. "But you know, it's worked up until now."

Charles Travis's solution to every problem was to work harder. This was also the solution he expected from his employees. He was very loyal to the people who had been with him from the beginning, giving them increased responsibilities far beyond their level of experience, and unfortunately, sometimes beyond their level of ability. But he steadfastly refused to build an experienced management team.

His wake-up call came when exploding sales caused the overworked back-office to fall two months behind in its billing. Obviously, when there are no bills being sent out, you are not getting paid. This $80 million company suffered a severe cash crunch because there was no manager in charge of this unit to authorize the hiring of a few additional people in the billing department.

Travis Housewares' problem was its poor allocation of human resources. In this specific instance, it needed a few extra clerks in the billing department. But the *real* human resources problem was the missing management team and information system that would have identified the billing problem before it became a crisis.

Charles Travis's hesitancy to hire experienced managers went beyond the inclination to spend his capital on directly revenue-producing items. Like many entrepreneurs, he knew that he *needed* a team, but he was trapped in his early hiring behavior.

In the early days of a start-up, it is not essential to define job requirements or set up performance evaluations. Charles hired people he liked for vaguely defined duties, and if they didn't work out, he fired them. He couldn't pay salaries at the high end of the spectrum, which meant he did not always attract top candidates. But since the business was small, and he kept his finger on its pulse, this worked out fine. Training took place on an ad hoc basis, which essentially meant there was no training.

But as a business expands, three human resources problems start to emerge.

First, the business may expand faster than employees' skill levels. Charles stuck by his early hires even when their newly expanded duties went far beyond their abilities. This resulted in many missed opportunities, embarrassments, and frustration for the employees themselves, who often turned out to be in over their heads.

It also nearly cost the company a great deal of money. Charles had an accountant who'd been with the company from the very beginning. She was young, and very loyal, and she'd made a lot of personal sacrifices for the company. When the IRS announced they were going to audit the company's tax returns, Charles' accountant decided to handle it herself. She met with the IRS agent at the company's offices. Only after the agent was ready to issue a preliminary assessment of three quarters of a million dollars in back taxes, penalties, and interest did Charles realize what a serious problem he had on his hands. His young employee had committed two cardinal errors in handling an IRS audit: She'd tried to handle the audit on her own, rather than hire an expert, and she'd allowed the agent onto the company's premises.

Second, without good job descriptions worked out in advance, and an understanding of adequate salary requirements, expanding companies can very easily hire the wrong people. When Charles *did* hire outsiders, he didn't stop to define the specific requirements of the job or find out how much he would have to pay to attract top candidates. He had no training program to get them up to speed, and no scheduled performance evaluations to let them know how they were doing. Because of this, the new hires were sometimes as ill prepared for what was in store for them as the old ones had been. Charles was unhappy, the employees were unhappy, and turnover in the accounting and finance department was high.

Third, expanding companies tend to stick with the management structure they know, rather than implement a new one to control their growing organization. Like many entrepreneurs, Charles kept the exact same management structure he'd used from the very beginning—he just added on to it piece by piece. When we asked to see the Travis Housewares Company's organizational chart, it consisted of two lines: the president on the first line, and twenty people on the second line all reporting to the president. While this had worked well in the early days, this structure had now become totally unwieldy.

Entrepreneurs always have rationales for why a management team might not be a good idea for them. One of our favorites is the argument that a company may hire too *many* people and end up with a top-heavy bureaucracy incapable of fast action. Charles made this case to us one night in his cramped office. Every horizontal surface of the room was covered with several inches of printouts, papers, correspondence, and prototypes of new household products—the result of one individual trying to stay in control of a huge company without any infrastructure. "I'm afraid we'll lose our competitive edge," he kept saying.

Charles is a great man, but his fears of going too far in the other direction were somewhat exaggerated. In our experience, entrepreneurs almost never do. These are people who feel that any company expenditure is really coming directly out of their own pockets. Entrepreneurial start-ups are, after all, *not* big institutional firms with massive budgets that are likely to get out of hand. And what's more, they'll never get the *chance* to become huge institutional firms either—unless they hire competent people, give them an organizational structure to work within, and then give up enough control to let them do their jobs.

## DELEGATE, DELEGATE, DELEGATE

Of course, control is often a real sticking point. Entrepreneurs usually feel that they did not get where they are today by giving up control to anybody. They've succeeded by being hands-on, and this behavioral pattern—the result of years of positive reinforcement—is hard to change.

Take Katherine Briggs, the founder and CEO of House Fashion, a designer and manufacturer of women's clothing. Katherine had been in the sales end of the apparel business for years before deciding to go out on her own. Unlike many entrepreneurs, Katherine listened to her friends' advice and invested early on in a good information system. She also hired a highly qualified CFO, and as the business grew over 10 years, she created new divisions to handle new product lines. Each division was run by a vice president. In other words, Katherine was doing a lot of things right.

But Katherine also kept most of the decision making, and much of the company's information, to herself. For example, her vice presidents never received useful management information for their divisions. The vice presidents' experience, like her own, was in sales, and sales drove the company. To keep the sales volume growing, Katherine invested heavily in product design and customer support.

Product design is never easy to control. Even experienced managers have difficulty assessing how much to invest in this area. But Katherine did not put a manager in charge of the company's 40-person design team. In theory, Katherine herself was in charge—but she was often out of the country visiting suppliers, thus leaving the design department to manage itself. And product design is an area that does not exactly lend itself to self-policing.

To achieve even higher sales, prices were cut as well. The company's CFO became worried. With all the growth in payroll and overhead, any further deterioration of profit margins could be devastating. The CFO was also concerned that the company's new bonus system, which was based solely on sales rather than on profits, didn't encourage managers to look at the bottom line—even if Katherine had been willing to show it to them.

Katherine overruled the CFO. She was on the road during most of this period, trying to solve some production problems overseas, and she didn't have a lot of time to review the financial reports. The result was that as business softened, Katherine was caught flat-footed. The company did not meet its budget and ended the year with a loss, at which point the banks stepped in and threatened to take over the company.

As a rule, entrepreneurs are very hesitant to delegate. Even when they know they're too busy to pay attention to all the areas and details of the business, there is still the impulse not to give up any control. We were present at a meeting when the founder of a company learned that one of his executives had commissioned a study without consulting him. He pounded on a table and then yelled into this highly paid professional's ear, "I've told you this before: no independent thinking!" Unfortunately, he wasn't kidding.

In part, delegating authority is difficult because if a mistake is going to be made, the entrepreneur feels more comfortable if it is his or her mistake. Entrepreneurs are also afraid that they will lose control if they aren't involved in all aspects of the business. This is one reason why we see owners of $50-million-plus businesses still opening the mail every morning.

When the entrepreneur overcomes these issues and does hire outside management, he or she will often doubt the manager's ability. One of our clients hired a marketing manager to develop sales and marketing programs that would attract new customers. The manager spent a considerable amount of time researching the company's products, customer needs, and the marketplace. He developed a number of excellent recommendations, which he presented to the owner.

The owner listened carefully, then explained why he thought none of the marketing manager's ideas would work. Instead, he told the manager what should be done. In one 10-minute meeting, the owner transformed his high-powered marketing manager from a creative executive into a high-priced secretary. The manager consulted the owner on all future decisions, and the owner eventually decided that this manager was "my kind of guy" after all. Of course, the creative input the manager had been hired to give had been completely stifled by the owner's inability to let go.

That reluctance to let go can survive long after common sense would indicate that it is no longer working. Even in the aftermath of House Fashion's big loss, the owner rejected the idea of hiring a chief operating officer to oversee production, design, and other areas of the company. "What does he know?," Katherine asked. "If he's so smart why doesn't he have his own company?"

Answering this question goes a long way to describing what this book is all about, because the talents of a good manager are, by nature, often quite different from the talents of an entrepreneur. As we said in our preface, an entrepreneur's genius, drive, and determination—what made the company possible in the first place—do not necessarily lend themselves to the creation of infrastructure. By the same token, a good manager's abilities to build an organization and systems capable of handling exponential growth do not necessarily lend themselves to the creation of a start-up company. But the combination of a gifted entrepreneur and a gifted manager can produce impressive results indeed.

To answer Katherine's implicit question: no, a chief operating officer could not take the place of the entrepreneur. If the COO's talents lay in that direction, he probably *would* be off starting his own company. But hiring a chief operating officer and/or a CFO and/or a management team will free up the entrepreneur to do what she does best—sell, create, and strategize.

## THE IMPORTANCE OF PEOPLE

When Charles Travis found out his company temporarily had no money in the till because the billing department was a month behind, he went down to talk to the billing personnel on the second floor. Below, you'll find two versions of his opening remarks to the department:

A. "Listen, I've ordered in some food for later, but right now, is there anything I can do to help you all? Do we need to hire more people?"

B. "Are you all stupid, or are you just lazy? Do *any* of you know what you're doing?"

Choice B is a direct quote.

Many entrepreneurs fail to understand the emotional needs of their employees, or the potential benefits of motivational tools. Of course, a paycheck is a motivational tool in its own right, but even small gestures of appreciation such as a simple "thank you" can go a long way to building company morale.

Charles Travis could not have chosen a worse tone if he tried. If what he really wanted to accomplish was to get his billing department to stay late and work harder, choice A would clearly have worked better.

As a business expands, formal performance evaluations and periodic feedback become more important. When the number of employees increases, the entrepreneur will not be able to track everyone's performance personally. Evaluations are a key part of the information systems that will help him to stay in control of a much larger organization.

Professional managers are generally much more adept than entrepreneurs at giving positive reinforcement and constructive criticism and at maintaining frequent two-way communication—all of which give employees a sense of belonging and encourage them to take an ownership role in their jobs.

One of our clients recently hired a human resources manager. The new manager's first order of business was to survey the company employees to determine their perceptions and feelings about the company. The manager's survey revealed that the employees were fairly happy with their work situation, although each had various individual complaints. But there was one point on which they virtually all agreed: they wanted the company to provide matching funds to their 401(K) contributions. This came through so clearly in the initial reports of the survey that the company acted even before the survey had been completed. It required a relatively small investment on behalf of the company, yet went a long way toward addressing the needs of the employees. The employees were not simply satisfied because the company had helped them financially; they were also extremely gratified to have been consulted.

Employees in general are motivated by appreciation, financial reward, opportunity, and challenge. But often it is small things that need to be achieved to keep people happy and make the workplace fun.

## NO PLANS FOR THE FUTURE

When a company expands, it is a signal that the company believes it has a future. For many entrepreneurs, however, the future looks very much like the present. This is not surprising: The entrepreneur's focus is traditionally on the short term. Initially, he wants to make sure his concept works. Then, once the concept is a success, he wants to maximize short-term profits.

Bear in mind that there has often been a significant delay in the entrepreneur's gratification. Several false starts, long lags in initial manufacturing, and a dearth of marketing capital may all have contributed to the slow start of a new product.

The entrepreneur wants to expand, but the model in his mind's eye is often based on a replica of his original success, only bigger. The need for an entirely new model, or even for extensive modifications to his original plan, is not something that the typical entrepreneur wants to face.

Left to his own devices, he will stay with vendors long after he's outgrown them and make no use of benchmarking (the practice of comparing your company to other well-run companies) to see where the company needs to focus its efforts. He will avoid new arenas, and tend to dismiss external events that may affect his markets.

Whenever we think about long-term planning, we always think about BL Thompson, an earth-moving company out in Montana. Tommy Thompson is the epitome of the successful entrepreneur. Moving hundreds of thousands of tons of dirt is dangerous, rough work, and Tommy can have his rough edges as well. But as every one of his employees would attest, the boss has a heart of gold. At BL Thompson, even low-level employees receive stock options. The result is a loyal staff with almost no turnover, and an outstanding safety record. The company credo is to do it right the first time, and treat the customer with dignity. In highway construction and mining circles, the reputation of the company is unparalleled.

The real genius of these people lies in their ability to market the type of company they are—a family-run company that believes in quality—in a business that doesn't generally favor companies that market themselves. In earth-moving, it's usually the low bid that gets the job, but BLT made people forget about the rock-bottom line.

However, the Thompson Company had reached a plateau at sales of $50 million. They were the best at what they did, but try as they might, Tommy and his managers couldn't seem to grow the company any bigger. The bulk of their business was in highway construction, although they had made small forays into mining, the railroad industry, and the power generation industry. Their problem, as they discussed it with us, was that the highway construction business is a very low margin enterprise. As a result, their profits were being eroded. Many jobs are awarded based on bids, which forces bidders to cut prices to the bone. What BL Thompson needed was a plan for growth and expansion.

Strategic planning—the process by which businesses examine their strengths and weaknesses and devise plans for both their short-term and long-term growth—is the key to real expansion. By searching out new markets and new opportunities, could they segue out of the highway construction business and into more profitable venues for earth-moving? You'll find the rest of BL Thompson's story, along with a complete description of how the entrepreneur can make use of strategic planning, in the next chapter.

## THE INEFFECTIVE IMPLEMENTATION OF SYSTEMS AND TECHNOLOGY

When a business is small, the owner can afford the luxury of visiting all the work sites. He is operating as much by "gut feeling" as by hard numbers. He can walk into a warehouse and actually see and touch the inventory. Entrepreneurs are often reluctant to abandon this visceral approach to their businesses, even when the businesses have grown so large that it is not physically possible for one person to visit all the sites. They feel that they will lose control of the business. Of course, an effective information system can provide the owner with the same (or better) information than he received when he did physical inspections. But try telling that to someone who has never relied on an information system before.

Entrepreneurs often think of information systems as back-office expenses that usurp capital clearly needed for revenue-producing items—when in fact the right information system can actually generate revenue as well. For example, take the case of Wal-Mart, a company that has made major investments in systems. Let's suppose that Wal-Mart's private-label green sweatshirts aren't selling in Bentonville, Arkansas. The manager in charge of green sweatshirts looks at his computer and realizes that while he can't seem to give them away in Bentonville, green sweatshirts are big sellers in Austin, Texas.

So the manager immediately ships every green sweatshirt from Bentonville to Austin, and instead of having to mark that sweatshirt down from $20 to $10 in Arkansas, he's able to sell it for $22 in Texas because demand is so heavy.

Systems tell you where your opportunities are and where your challenges lie. They can even function as an early-warning system. Of course, just because you have an information system doesn't mean you're getting good information. This was a lesson LJ Electronics learned when it almost went bankrupt by underestimating the costs of its charge-backs and volume rebates. LJ Electronics' executives made the classic information system mistake: They bought their hardware before their software.

Here's the way it typically happens. The head of the company meets a salesman from a large maker of computers. He knows he needs an information system—his CFO is talking of nothing else—so he goes for it. He buys the computers. Then, he and his CFO start shopping for software to run on the computers. Unfortunately, it turns out that the software they'd really like to buy doesn't run on those computers, or that each machine will need to have its memory upgraded, at a high cost. Well, never mind, they've come this far, so they buy the upgrades. With hardware and software in hand, the company finally starts to think about what its informational needs actually are, and it turns out that the brand new software doesn't allow them to do some basic task the people in accounts receivable absolutely need.

LJ Electronics' rudimentary information system wasn't up to keeping track of a rapidly expanding company, but it was just solid enough to lull its CEO into a false sense of security.

## BREAKING DOWN THE WALL

Almost every expanding company hits the wall at some point. It happens at the point where hard work can no longer take the place of a missing infrastructure.

Breaking down that wall means breaking some old habits, but it can be done. In the following chapters you'll see how some of the companies we've profiled here have attempted it, and how you can too.

We'll show you how to build your team; how to find, retain, and reward good people; how to create a strategic plan; how to develop an effective information reporting system; how to keep on top of technology; how to prepare for business successions; how to form a board of directors; and finally, how to stay on top of the legal issues all this entails.

Just as important, we'll show you how each of these companies found ways to take a business structure and make it their own. A business plan that does not incorporate a business' personality and culture will ultimately not work.

An investment in infrastructure provides the framework to identify and deal with problems before they become critical. It enables a company to more effectively identify and take advantage of long-term opportunities. It allows a company to produce the kind of meaningful and timely financial reports that encourage investors and lenders to write checks.

It's also the only way we know to get past the wall.

## ENTREPRENEUR'S SUMMARY

A rapidly expanding entrepreneurial company's focus naturally tends to be on sales and production. With limited capital to spend, these companies put a lower priority on infrastructure: building an organization, putting a management team in place, and creating an information system. However, in our experience, a company can grow only so far without these components in place. In this chapter, we discussed the typical problems that face a growing entrepreneurial company.

These problems include:

1. *The ineffective deployment of human resources.* Without a management team, a company will be unable to respond fast enough to new opportunities, and will miss warning signs of trouble. There are three things in particular to look out for as a business expands: (i) the business may grow faster than employees' skill levels; (ii) without good job descriptions worked out in advance, and an understanding of adequate salary requirements, expanding companies can very easily

hire the wrong people; and (iii) expanding companies tend to stick with the management structure they know, rather than making the necessary changes and adjustments as the organization grows.

2. *The typical entrepreneur's hesitancy to delegate.* The skills needed to propel a new business to success are quite different from the skills necessary to grow an established business. As the business grows, the entrepreneur can't do it all himself. He must learn to hand over some control to trusted managers.

3. *A lack of appreciation of the importance of "people issues."* Of course, correct compensation levels are critical, but many entrepreneurs underestimate the value of even small gestures of appreciation toward their employees. The potential benefits of motivational tools are incalculable.

4. *The lack of long-term planning.* An entrepreneurial company typically focuses on day-to-day operations without looking ahead. Strategic planning—the process by which businesses examine their strengths and weaknesses and devise plans for both their short-term and long-term growth—is the key to real expansion.

5. *The ineffective implementation of systems and technology.* Entrepreneurs need to keep their hand on the pulse of their business. In the beginning, of course, this means being involved in every decision, actually being able to visit all sites on a regular basis, and actually seeing the customer and touching the product. However, as a business expands, it becomes necessary to set up an information system that will give the entrepreneur the same ability on a much larger scale. An information system can tell you where your opportunities are and where your challenges lie, and function as an early-warning system when things are not going according to plan.

# Developing a Strategic Plan

"You don't have to change . . . survival is not
mandatory."
—W. Edwards Deming

## THE STRATEGIC PLANNING PROCESS

Few topics have received more attention in the business press over
the years than strategic planning. Nearly all business schools offer
courses or whole curricula centered around this topic. Many books
have been written; thousands of workshops and seminars have been
held; entire companies—the so-called "strategy boutiques"—have
been created to help businesses plan strategically.

So you would think by now that the idea of, and need for, strategic planning would be pretty well understood and disseminated.
Well, let us take you back for a moment to LJ Electronics, the consumer
electronics company we described in the previous chapter.

When CEO and founder Larry Jones brought us in to help after
LJ Electronics' brush with disaster, we asked at one of our first meetings if he'd done any strategic planning.

"Oh, sure," Larry said, pulling out a bound report. "Here it is."
The report turned out to be an operating plan; basically his budget
for next year. We pointed out that this was an operating plan for
next year. "Well, what do you mean by strategic plan?" asked Larry,
puzzled.

Strategic planning is the process of deciding where you want to

Exhibit 2-1
Strategic Planning—Introduction

## A process which creates a common vision
## and common goals for an organization

*Without*                    *With*

go and how you're going to get there (See Exhibit 2-1). It's about the creation of new products and the expansion of new markets; it's about getting rid of unproductive current products and exiting selected markets. And it's the most effective method anyone has come up with so far to competitively position your company for the future—because above all, strategic planning is about the future.

What does it take to plan for the future? Patience, commitment, rigorous fact-finding, teamwork, honesty, and—at a minimum—calendars. If you think we're kidding, come with us to the Acme Egg Company.

Acme Egg was built by Joe Johnson, who literally started with a couple of chickens and a barn. Over the course of 10 years, he'd taken those chickens and hatched himself a $30-million-a-year business. And that's where he'd been stuck for the previous several years. We drove out to his operation in rural Pennsylvania and he took us on a tour. We found immaculate barns with state-of-the-art egg equipment. Then we went into the offices, which looked like they came straight out of the 19th century. All transactions were still being recorded on paper. There were maybe a couple of computers, but no comprehensive information system at all. He and his back office staff came in each day to do *that* day's work—that was their plan. Whatever fires came up that day, they put out that day, but there was a lot of resistance to looking forward a year or two years.

We sat down and started trying to match dates with key goals they had developed. That's when we discovered that none of the managers had calendars.

Of course, most companies aren't as extreme examples as Acme Egg. Most companies engage in some type of planning, such as financial planning, new product planning, succession planning, systems planning, etc. But strategic planning isn't about one part of the company; it's about the whole company. Strategic planning is the umbrella plan that provides a context for all the other plans.

In the strategic-planning process, a company analyzes its strengths and weaknesses and examines current and potential opportunities. Based on this information, the company develops strategy for itself (See Exhibit 2-2). That strategy then becomes the basis for supporting strategies for its various departments. Goals are set and a review process is instituted to trouble-shoot, update the goals, and revalidate assumptions—in other words, to make sure that something actually happens.

This is where all too many strategic plans go astray—at implementation. Business management surveys show that most CEOs who have a strategic plan are concerned with the potential breakdown in the implementation of the plan. Without implementation, strategic plans don't gather momentum. They gather dust. We know. We've

**Exhibit 2-2**
Strategic Situation

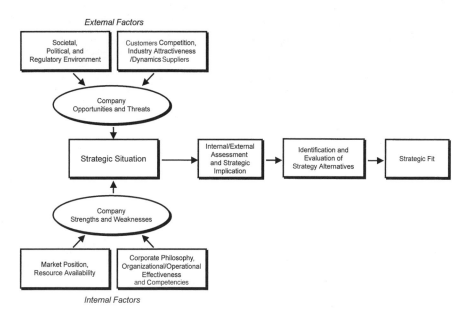

literally seen the dust gathering on great big vinyl binders stuffed with fancy strategic plans that nobody ever reads.

Why don't strategic plans get implemented? In our experience it's usually because accountability for the implementation hasn't been built into the plan and no review process has been set up to ensure implementation.

There's one other reason that plans gather dust: lack of owner-ship. A company has to *own* its plan. Outsiders can help facilitate the process, but in the final analysis, if the company doesn't make the plan, the company won't follow the plan. This was one of the prob-lems with strategic planning in the 1980s. In that era, it was an ab-stract, top-down process. Number-crunching experts came into a company and generated tome-like volumes filled with grand theories that had little to do with the day-to-day realities of the company. Only the most senior managers were involved; lower level manage-ment often wasn't consulted. Neither were the company's customers. No wonder many of these plans languished, unused. Strategic plan-ning has to include a wide range of people, from line managers to customers to suppliers.

This can be easier said than done. Take the LJ Electronics Com-pany. The company was built around Larry Jones's imagination and creative drive. When we told him we wanted to interview the employ-ees of LJ Electronics, he said, "Why? I think I know what my company needs." His vision had gotten the company this far, he figured, so why did he need anyone else's opinion? We've learned that working with an entrepreneurial CEO is a delicate balancing act.

If the CEO isn't on board and behind the plan, you might as well forget it. But if he doesn't allow other people into the process, then he's going to confront the same limitations that are keeping him stuck at his current revenue level. The CEO wants his company to grow; he just doesn't want his company to change. And growth with-out change is obviously difficult. From his point of view, it makes sense: Why change a formula that's worked so far? The trick is to show him that strategic planning isn't destroying what he's made; it's building on what he's already created. Ironically, once an entrepre-neur gets on board, he'll often be the plan's biggest cheerleader. It's a matter of making him see the need and the benefits. And there's no question that there are benefits.

A recent survey queried just under one thousand small-to-medium-sized businesses to compare companies with a strategic plan to companies without one. The survey found that companies with written strategic plans had 100% higher profits than the other companies. The companies with strategic plans had annual revenue growth of 6.2% as opposed to 3.8% for the other companies. But the benefits of strategic planning go beyond these statistics.

Here's a short list of the most common *proven* results of the strategic planning process: increased revenues, increased profits, improved resource allocation, improved customer satisfaction, enhanced employee morale, and improved return on investment and assets. Strategic planning helps companies communicate their goals to all their employees. It helps companies differentiate themselves from the competition. And, perhaps most importantly, a strategic plan helps companies anticipate—and survive—change.

Change, after all, is the business background music all of us are dancing to. We live in an information age and we do business in a global economy. New technology and the mobility of capital mean that things change faster than ever before. "What's the point of planning for the future when the future changes so rapidly?" some businesses ask. Why bother planning two years ahead when market dynamics could change by next quarter? But the fact is, it's the very pace of change that makes planning more important than ever. No company, no matter what kind of business they're in, or how long they've been in it, can assume that the conditions they're operating in now will stay the same. And no company has unlimited resources to use while meandering in this environment.

In other words, it's no longer business as usual for anyone. Now, more than ever, companies have to stay alert to changes in the marketplace, changes in technology, and changes in the regulatory and financial environments. And they need a way to position themselves relative to those changes. In an environment of continual and rapid change, long-range planning expands your options and organizational flexibility.

## THE FIVE PHASES TO STRATEGIC PLANNING

We quoted W. Edwards Deming at the head of this chapter, but lots of business books quote Deming, so we're also going to quote Woody

Allen. As Mr. Allen put it in one of his movies, "Relationships are like sharks; if they don't move forward, they die." We would add one more category to the list of things that have to move forward: businesses. If you're doing business today, you'd better be moving forward. And if you're moving forward, you obviously need to know where you're going.

We've worked with hundreds of companies of all sizes and shapes in virtually all sectors of the U.S. economy, and we've learned that successful organizations follow a similar strategic planning and implementation process. This is the process we want to share with you (See Exhibit 2-3).

As we practice it, there are five phases to strategic planning: internal assessment of your business; external assessment of the marketplace; management/leadership planning sessions, where the company's team gathers together to come up with a vision or plan for the future; the implementation of that plan; and reassessment of how the execution of the plan is going.

Although we've just described it in five neat linear phrases, strategic planning is a creative process—and like any creative process, it's dependent on the human factor. It takes shape differently in every organization and even differently from year to year within the same organization.

That said, here's how it usually goes.

**Exhibit 2-3**
Strategic Planning—An Integrated Process

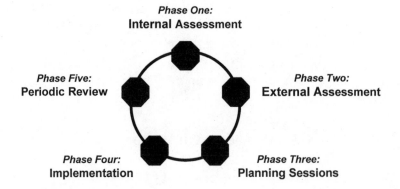

*Phase One:*
**Internal Assessment**

*Phase Five:*
**Periodic Review**

*Phase Two:*
**External Assessment**

*Phase Four:*
**Implementation**

*Phase Three:*
**Planning Sessions**

**Exhibit 2-4**
Issues to Consider When Assessing the Current Situation

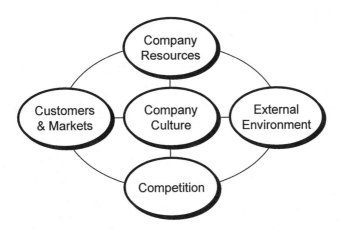

## Phase One: Internal Assessment—Where Are We Now?

One way to look at the strategic planning process is as a series of questions. Naturally, since a strategic plan is a kind of road map to the future, the very first question to ask is: Where are we now?

To answer this question, a company has to ask itself: What are our strengths and weaknesses? What are we good at? What are our competencies? What do we perceive to be our key long-range issues and opportunities? And how are we doing right now?

"How are we doing right now?" means a number of things (See Exhibit 2-4). It means identifying all the company's critical processes: for example, product development, order fulfillment, and customer service—each element of the business pipeline. The company must then ask: How good *are* we at product development? How *well* are we fulfilling orders? And then it has to decide how important each of these processes is to the company.

If a process is important, and is not being performed well, it's obviously essential to target that process for improvement. For instance, if a company judges that product development is a critical item, but acknowledges that it has poor product development, then that area becomes a top priority.

And of course, the company managers have to look at the bottom line. Where are they making money? And where are they losing money? Just as important as these "hard line" business questions is another "softer" one: Who are we as a company and what do we believe in? Any solution to a business problem, any plan for the future, has to take this into account.

That was the situation at Paper Ink, Inc., a privately held paper and packaging company we worked with. The owner of Paper Ink was kind of a remarkable man: He believed in maximizing employment, regardless of how it affected revenue. He even set up programs in prisons for prisoners to fold boxes so they could learn work skills. This didn't bring in much revenue, and it generated a lot of bureaucratic paperwork, but the owner was committed to doing what he felt was the right thing. Any plan for this company's future had to take the owner's values into account. Outside consultants might wring their hands at some of his business principles, but these principles were part of the culture of the company.

In the kinds of entrepreneurial businesses we're discussing here, the values of the company are often the values of the person at the top, so it's crucial to get that person behind the plan. This may seem obvious but all too often we've seen plans come to nothing because the CEO wasn't behind the plan. If the plan doesn't "belong" to the CEO and his team, then it has no chance to succeed.

There's one other key question in the assessment phase. And that's to ask: What *was* our plan?

Which brings us back to the BL Thompson Company. We described this old Montana family firm in the previous chapter. BLT is an earth-moving company; it specializes in highway construction with a little mining thrown in. The CEO is Tommy Thompson, a self-made man in his sixties. Tommy had taken the company from revenues of $10 million to $50 million, but now pre-tax profits were sagging. Tommy wanted the company to grow but when we advised him to think about strategic planning, he resisted the idea.

"Why do I need to do this?" he asked.

"Did you ever have a vision for the company?" we asked.

"To make this a $50-million-a-year business," said Tommy.

The company had already reached that milestone.

"Great. What's your new vision?," we asked.

There was dead silence for a very long 10 seconds. When that

24

10 seconds was over, Tommy broke into a grin. He'd finally seen the need for a strategic plan.

BL Thompson, in fact, is almost a classic example of what strategic planning can do for a company.

There are nine Thompsons working in the firm, but there's no question in anyone's mind that the firm is Tommy's. Tommy grew up during World War II and can be, as his employees told us, "one tough son of a bitch." But he is also very kindhearted, exceedingly gracious, and willing to lose money in order to do the right thing.

The company reflects his values. Dirt moving, which is basically what BLT does, is a dangerous, transient business. People have to move to where the dirt is and it's hard on families. Tommy allowed many employees to buy stock in the company, a practice virtually unheard of in the construction business. They had a reputation for doing things right the first time.

As part of our assessment, we collected and organized information on markets, business performance, finances, and the current company organization (who reported to whom). Then we did interviews with management and a cross section of employees. These people had some impressive strengths. They were willing to undertake risky jobs; they had good relationships with their customers and subcontractors; they were good at estimating jobs; they had a proven ability to get the jobs they wanted; they had the right equipment—and a much better than average work force.

Another strength, and one that would prove critical to the company's future, was that they were entrepreneurial; they were willing to try new things. In its strengths as in so much else, the company reflected Tommy's values.

But they also had weaknesses. They didn't know much about the market or their competitors; they didn't have a marketing process (a way to find and sell themselves to new markets); their estimators were doubling as project managers and were spread too thin; and they didn't have a developed criteria for selecting projects.

We learned something else during our internal assessment: the company's profit margins on the bulk of their work—in highway construction—were very low. Their profit margins on mining operations—a sideline business—were much higher. No wonder they were stalled out.

In fact, BLT's low profit margins proved to be the key insight into turning around their growth. If the company did more of the high-profit-margin mining work and less of the low-profit-margin highway work, they'd be making more money. But how could they get more mining work? Was there room in the mining market for them? And were there other markets with even higher profit margins for them to explore? BL Thompson was ready for Phase Two.

## Phase Two: External Assessment—What's Out There?

No one can plan for the future in a vacuum. Besides looking inward to your company's strengths and weaknesses, you have to look outward as well, to the marketplace your company operates in. What are your competitors up to? What do your customers want? And what new markets can you enter? These are some of the key questions in Phase Two (See Exhibit 2-5).

When investigating the marketplace, companies usually *do* check out the competition. In fact, competitive pressures are often the impetus behind a company's desire to create a strategic plan. But it's not enough to look over your shoulder to see who's gaining on you. You also have to look over to your side—where your customers are. After all, you're in business to serve your customers' needs. If you aren't talking to your customers, you're missing an important piece of the puzzle.

Tommy was so relationship-oriented that he was almost embarrassed to go to his customers. He said, "I'm supposed to *know* what they want already." We stressed that we were going to be talking to them in order to find out what they wanted *even better*.

And what the customers said was really surprising: price was not the most important thing when it comes to earth-moving. The

**Exhibit 2-5**
External Factors

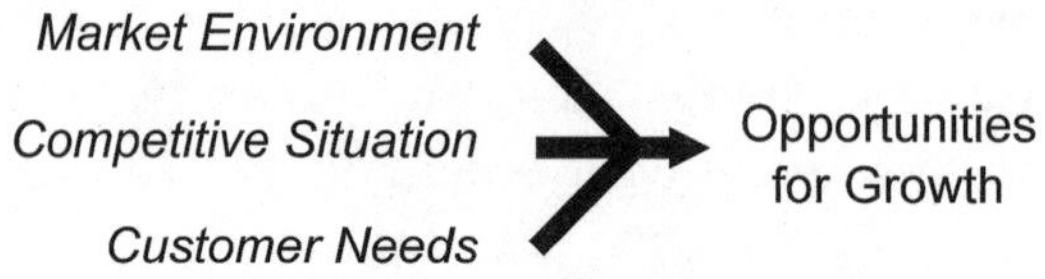

Market Environment

Competitive Situation  ➤  Opportunities for Growth

Customer Needs

most critical concern, according to these customers, was to do it safely, to staff it correctly, to schedule it quickly. Speed was essential in most of their markets—the clients wanted it done quickly and done correctly. That was BLT's specialty, and we began to see that there was a lot of demand out there that hadn't been tapped.

There's one other place to look—to the future. What new markets are there for your company? And in today's economy, you can't just think domestically. For more and more American companies, the international market has become as important as the domestic one. In fact, according to the 1996 Grant Thornton Survey of American Manufacturers, the dollar volume of U.S. exports has increased some 50% since 1990.

Finding new markets was the turning point for the management of BL Thompson. They were used to thinking of themselves as a highway construction company, although they did earth-moving for various other industries. But once they realized how low their highway construction profit margins were, they decided not to make it a strategic priority. Market research indicated that the region they were accustomed to working in couldn't accommodate much expansion. So, they decided to do additional research into other markets: the southwestern construction industry, the railroad industry (rail companies need lots of earth moved), and the power-generation market (which requires large drainage and holding ponds).

The BL Thompson story is a classic example of how an internal and external assessment—Phases One and Two—dovetail to generate a new direction. The company asked itself what its old vision had been and acknowledged that it had already been achieved. The new goal was to grow even bigger. So the management of BL Thompson looked at their critical processes, and discovered that what they did, they did well; they just didn't make enough money doing it. They identified their competency as earth-moving and asked themselves where additional markets for this expertise could be found. Their ultimate decision was to pursue non-highway work, which offered the prospect of more growth.

But looking for new markets also means "thinking outside the box." Let's return for a moment to Paper Ink, Inc. Paper Ink was losing money and their parent company was losing patience. Did that mean that the general manager was meeting with his team to develop a strategy? No.

So we met with the general manager and his four-man team—the heads of marketing, finance, operations, and creative advertising, and challenged them to think about the problem without any preconceptions. Clearly, the company needed to be "recreated." It was time to throw away the rule book.

The company's internal assessment showed that their strength was direct marketing. Why not take that strength and get into *any* market where there was an opportunity? All sorts of ideas came up. The research that the team did on the direct-mail market showed a trend toward organic gardening. That was one idea. Other ideas for product catalogs were suggested: supplies for the mortuary market; batteries; mobile communications; and a resource catalog for builders and architects. The key was thinking outside the box.

### Phase Three: Management and Leadership Planning Sessions—Where Do We Want to Go?

This is the emotional heart and soul of the strategic-planning process. It's where all the introspection and investigation of the previous two phases come to fruition. It's where the elements of data and analysis get mixed together with the key ingredient—the human factor. When you take data and analysis and add the human factors—creativity and enthusiasm—you get a potent mix. That mix is the strategic plan.

Over the years, we've found it's often the case that our entrepreneur clients will see the need for a strategic plan but resist the idea of planning sessions or off-site retreats. "Why waste all that time away from the office?" they'll ask. There are several reasons for going off-site, and like most of what we're going to tell you about the retreat, they have to do with that all-important human factor.

For one thing, no one can concentrate when the phones are ringing and they're dealing with the daily minutiae of the office. For another, during a retreat you're challenging people to think in new ways, so you want to create an environment that's different from the familiar pell-mell of the office. Finally, you don't want to ignore one very important by-product of the retreat: team building. Over several days, as leaders discuss the strengths and weaknesses of what the company does, they put their personal differences aside. People get to know each other. Some of the ordinary interoffice rivalries and resentments tend to dissipate; the usual causes of conflict aren't present and everyone is working together toward the same goal. The team starts to gel.

In fact, watching the team come together is one of the most exciting aspects of strategic planning. When a retreat is properly organized and facilitated, it creates a feeling of ownership among the team members. Would it be possible to take all the research and interviews from Phases One and Two and sit down the CEO and come up with a plan? Of course. But you'd have to explain the vision to the key people in the company anyway, and they might resent or misunderstand it. When the team participates in the plan, working things out together, it creates psychic ownership among the team. Everyone knows the plan, remembers how it came about, and feels as if it's theirs. That's the kind of retreat the Thompson company had.

The Thompson retreat was held at an isolated resort in the north woods, a very rustic spot, with log cabins and moose heads over the fireplaces. It took place in January. Each retreat tends to have a different kind of atmosphere, depending on the corporate culture. But BL Thompson is a Marlboro Man kind of company. So the team went ice fishing and rode around on snowmobiles during breaks (See Exhibit 2-6).

Who exactly is on the team we keep referring to? The team is the group of key employees responsible for putting together and exe-

**Exhibit 2-6**
Inputs to the Planning Process

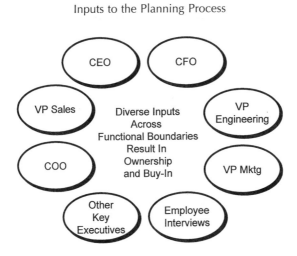

cuting the strategic plan. Besides the CEO, it should include the CFO; the COO; the vice presidents of marketing, sales, and engineering; and any other key executives. We recommend no more than ten people on a retreat team, although many more than that should be interviewed during Phases One and Two. That way, lower levels of management can make critically important contributions about the company's strengths and weaknesses. And interviewing them ensures a participative process anchored in the reality of how the company is operating. When we interviewed the Thompson Company employees, some people would ask us, "Hey, why are you interviewing *him*? He's just a truckdriver." But the people from the lower echelons sometimes have the best insights about how the company runs . . . and how it could run better.

The BL Thompson Company retreat had 9 people. The first three items on the agenda were: (1) What are our core values or ideology? (2) What's our vision for the year 2000? and (3) What are our growth strategies? Each member of the team had to come up with a "vision statement" to answer these questions. The vision statements covered the gamut—what they thought new markets would be; how big the company would grow; what their safety and risk management would be like.

Normally a very voluble guy, Tommy Thompson sat silently throughout the vision statements. He was waiting to see what his managers would say. Tommy wasn't entirely convinced that anyone other than him really had the right vision for the company. Did they see the company's mission the same way he did?

This attitude is not at all unusual for entrepreneurial CEOs. They're used to bulling ahead over the resistance of other people and relying solely on their own judgment. They're always surprised when they find out they don't have to go it alone.

As it turned out, the visions expressed at the Thompson retreat were very close to Tommy Thompson's; this is usually the mark of a well-run company. Tommy was pleased and surprised. The role of the CEO during a retreat is a tricky one. He's the boss and his views will—and should—lead the group. On the other hand, if he dominates the group from the start, the retreat becomes a meaningless exercise. One point of strategic planning in an entrepreneur-driven company is to bring new and different opinions to the fore.

That's why we always advise CEOs to speak *after* everyone else has had a turn. Even when this happens, lower management can be very cagey about expressing themselves in front of the boss. In this case, everyone felt comfortable speaking. Unfortunately, this is not always true.

One way to structure the opening vision statements so that team members speak openly is to do a "vision walk." Everyone writes down their thoughts on anonymous Post-Its and puts them up on a board. No one knows who wrote what. Then each point is discussed. If there's general consensus on a point, it stays on the board. The boss, of course, speaks last.

After the vision discussion, team members brainstorm a SWOT assessment. "SWOT" stands for Strengths, Weaknesses, Opportunities, and Threats. This should be kept simple—factual statements written in an easy-to-read presentation. Then strategies are defined in specific concise strategy statements, and goals are set and given target dates. For instance: "We're going to roll out three new products by 12/31/97 and Joe Smith is responsible as the goal owner to get that done."

The actual strategic planning document should be similarly concise. As we said before, a long fancy-bound tome isn't going to impress anyone but a stationer. It should be a succinct statement of the vision, the mission of the company, strategies, goals, and the assumptions about external factors such as the marketplace, competitors, the economy, and regulation. It might also include some internal assumptions about operations and the work force. The idea is to create something that you can read and remember.

Retreats often last several days, but there's no hard and fast rule. In fact, the Thompson retreat took place in two parts. After the first retreat, there was a one-month break. During this time, the team did some financial modeling and started to develop preliminary goals for the next year and preliminary marketing plans. Then they met again and translated the goals into first-year objectives. They took out a calendar and plotted out what would happen when.

Then they went back to the office to implement the plan.

## Phase Four: The Implementation Plan—How Are We Going to Get There?

It's great to have a goal and a vision but it doesn't count for much unless you have a way to translate it into action. That's what Phase

Four is about—creating a business plan and implementing it (See Exhibit 2-7).

Immediately following a retreat, there's a tendency for everyone to feel a little euphoric. After all, they've just emerged from an intense bonding experience and from this crucible they've forged a brilliant plan that will lead them to world domination in their market.

So a few weeks after the retreat, after everyone's "come down" off the retreat high, it's a good idea to hold a follow-up meeting. Does everyone feel okay about the goals? Can the company actually afford what it's planning to do? What resources—technology, capital, people—will be needed to meet the goals? This is where the dream meets the hard reality of the dollar and sometimes the plan has to be cut back. When this happens, the team has a tendency to blame the CFO for not getting behind the plan, but generally he's just being responsible. In this case, a resource allocation plan has to be developed to prioritize the goals.

Once the plan has been agreed on, detailed action plans have to be developed for each strategic goal, complete with timetables. An annual budget and calendar have to be created along with financial projections. What has to happen for the goals to be realized? Who's going to do it? By when? How much is it going to cost? Then, during the third quarter, planning for the next year should begin.

At BL Thompson, we asked everyone, "What are you going to be doing for the next year? And what do you need from the organization to be successful?" It took three months to put together an implementation plan. Then that plan was taken to all the current divisions of the company—finance, sales and marketing, human resources, etc. "Here's what we're planning to do in the next year," they were told. "What do you need in order to do your part of that?" Working all these details out took BLT another three months. (We told you at the beginning—strategic planning takes time, patience, and commitment.) The BLT plan called for reorganizing internally during the first

**Exhibit 2-7**
Keys to Success Implementation

| Clear Performance Objectives | Understanding of Investment Requirements | Timetables for Action | Access and Awareness |
| --- | --- | --- | --- |

year and developing new markets during the second year. It also called for a substantial investment in new machinery during the first year. The company deliberately took a hit during the first two years so they could double their profits in the third year.

One of the most common stumbling blocks to implementation of a strategic plan is access. No one can execute a plan he can't see. Everyone has to know what the plan is. We knew one CEO who posted his strategic planning retreat goals on his wall so he could literally "keep his eye on the goals" at all times. You don't have to do that, but one thing we do recommend is making the plan available to the entire organization. If the plan exists only as a fat book on a shelf, it won't get read and it won't get implemented.

Another potential pitfall is competition from within for resources needed to implement the plan. For instance, at BLT, there were several managers who were lobbying hard for additional capital expenditures in their divisions. When they were told funds weren't available, they said, "Without this money, we can't implement the plan." As bosses have done since the beginning of time, Tommy told them to implement it anyway, and they did. Tommy had the benefit of a lot of hard facts that had been developed before and during the retreat; he knew these divisions had adequate resources.

We've talked a lot about the human factor *during* the retreat, but it's just as vital in the planning phase. In other words, just as important as the "what, when, and how" is the "who."

BL Thompson asked us to do what they called a "management and leadership audit." It was clear to them that they were going to have to reorganize the company—something many businesses decide once they take a hard look at their infrastructure in the light of their mission. They wanted to have the right personnel in the right positions. We asked the 30 top managers to do what are called "360-degree surveys," in which management executives who work with each other write assessments of each other's performance. If it's done right, and kept utterly confidential, these surveys can be extremely valuable. Only the top four people at BLT got to read them.

At the time of the strategic plan, BLT was organized, like many companies, around its functions. There was a division for operations, a division for sales and marketing, a human resources division, a finance division.

This is the classic organizational business structure, and it had served BL Thompson well for many years. However, as a company diversifies and moves into new products and new markets, the functional model can become unwieldy, as each functional unit has to service several different products and markets. Tommy and his managers decided to organize instead around their markets.

Instead of dividing themselves into functional units, they organized themselves into what are called "strategic business units" (SBUs). Each unit was responsible only for one market. They formed a mining group, an earth-moving group, a railroad group, an energy and power engineering group, a waste and environmental group, and a heavy highway civil group. Within each group, there existed all the functional capabilities necessary to do business pretty much independently of every other group. The BLT management also formed a Finance and Administrative Services group to allocate funds and keep track of the other SBUs. We sometimes call this a "go to" organization: Instead of threading your way through a functional organization when you need something, you can simply "go to" mining or "go to" railroads. The Mining Unit is responsible for meeting the mining goals, the Railroad Unit is responsible for meeting the railroad goals. This kind of structure makes for better accountability. If you want to know how well the goals are being met in mining, it's easy—just go to the manager in charge of mining. It also makes for far greater efficiency. In effect, they now have several little companies, not just one big one.

Six months after the retreat, BLT had full implementation plans with performance objectives and investment requirements for the entire organization. Now, all they had to do was to keep doing the work.

## Phase Five: Review, Review, Review!

Strategic planning is not something you do just once: market conditions change, the competition changes, the financial and regulatory environments change. So it's essential to keep revalidating the assumptions of the plan during periodic reviews. These reviews should be held at a minimum of twice a year. Some companies hold them quarterly or even monthly. At these follow-up meetings, progress is measured and performances are evaluated. Problems that turn up can be dealt with. These follow-up meetings are also a good opportunity to communicate the new strategies to everyone (See Exhibit 2-8).

There can be a lot of obstacles to these meetings. If the company has an informal culture, and the team isn't used to meeting on a regular basis, there will often be some initial resistance. Sometimes an organization needs to appoint a "strategic nag"—someone on the inside who has enough clout to come in and nag everyone into executing the plan. The role of "strategic nag" can also be played by an outside consultant, provided that consultant has been empowered.

Often, the first time the team gets together for one of these reviews, some team members are embarrassed because they haven't accomplished anything yet. But we've found that by the second meeting more will have done their homework, and over time, as the reviews continue, the team will eventually start to embrace the plan. If finding time away from the hectic pace of the office is an obstacle, we suggest going off-site again.

**Exhibit 2-8**
Strategic Planning as a Management System—Functional Linkages

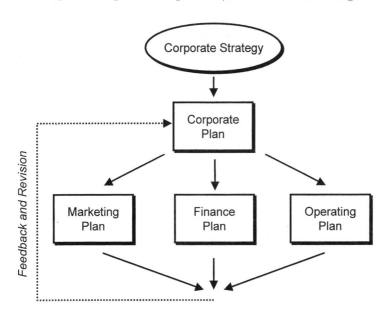

The value of these review meetings is inestimable, because no matter how carefully you plan in Phase Four, there's bound to be something you and your team didn't consider. And that something can hinder even the best-conceived and best-implemented plan.

Take what happened at Marcus Plastics, Inc., a plastics manufacturer. Their core business was manufacturing sheets of plastic but they also offered value-added plastic-processing services such as die cutting and sonic welding. Their primary business—manufacturing and selling the plastic sheets—had a very low profit margin. So they had decided to shift their business towards the higher margin operations of cutting and welding. They held a retreat, built a plan and a strategy—everything by the book.

Then nothing happened. The business went on exactly as it had before, with the low-margin plastic sheets accounting for most of their sales.

The management of Marcus was bewildered. Why weren't they increasing sales on the custom welding and cutting? At a review meeting, the problem turned up. They hadn't changed the incentives for the sales force. The salespersons were still making more money when they sold a plastic sheet than when they made a sale cutting or welding. Naturally, they weren't bothering to sell more of the new value-added products; it didn't make economic sense for them. Management redesigned the sales incentive program, and increased the commission on the processes.

Within a few months, Marcus Plastics no longer sold plastic sheets at all. The company now sells value-added plastic and their profits are way up. And believe us, they review quarterly.

As for the BL Thompson Company, Tommy figures he's 5 years away from gross revenues of $100 million. What will he do when he reaches it?

He'll just have to develop a new strategic plan.


## ENTREPRENEUR'S SUMMARY

To competitively position a company for the future, the management team must plan ahead to decide where they want the company to go and how it is going to get there. In the strategic-planning process, a company analyzes its strengths and weaknesses and examines current

### Exhibit 2-9
### Strategic Planning—Summary

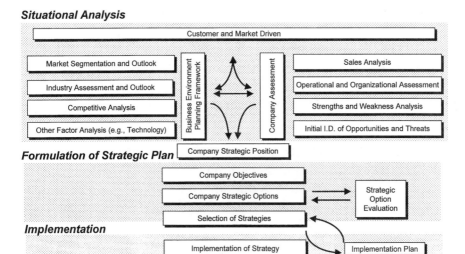

and potential opportunities. Based on this information, the company develops a strategy for itself (See Exhibit 2-9).

Some of the proven benefits of strategic planning are: increased revenues, increased profits, improved resource allocation, improved customer satisfaction, enhanced employee morale, and improved return on investment and assets. Strategic planning helps companies communicate their goals to all their employees. It helps companies differentiate themselves from the competition. And perhaps most importantly, a strategic plan helps companies anticipate—and survive—change.

There are five phases to strategic planning:

1. *An internal assessment of the company.* Before a business can make a plan for its future, the management team has to ask itself: What are our strengths and weaknesses? What are we good at? What are our competencies? What do we perceive to be our key long-range issues and opportunities? And how are we doing right now? The company managers also have to look at the bottom line. Where are we making money? And where are we losing money? Just as important as these "hard

line" business questions is another "softer" one: "Who are we as a company and what do we believe in?"

2. *External assessment of the marketplace.* No one can plan for the future in a vacuum. Besides looking inward to your company's strengths and weaknesses, you have to look outward as well, to the marketplace your company operates in. What are your competitors up to? What do your customers want? And what new markets can you enter?

3. *Management/leadership planning sessions.* This is where the company's team gathers together to come up with a vision or plan for the future. In meetings often held off-site, the management team looks at the data and analysis gathered in Phases One and Two and comes up with long-range goals for the company: the strategic plan itself.

4. *Implementation of the strategic plan.* After a plan has been agreed upon, it must be realized. In follow-up meetings, detailed plans have to be developed for each strategic goal—complete with timetables and budgets. This is where the dream meets the hard reality of the dollar, and companies must decide what resources—technology, capital, people—will be needed to meet the goals.

5. *Periodic reassessment of strategic goals.* It is essential to keep revalidating the assumptions of a company's strategic plan during periodic reviews. These reviews should be held at a minimum of twice a year. During these meetings, progress is measured, performances are evaluated, and the company's goals are reassessed in the light of an ever-changing business climate.

# Building Your Team

Any experienced manager would agree: The most important assets of a company are the people who work there. But without some kind of organizational structure into which to put them, the most talented individuals in the world will remain just that: individuals.

It might not seem like much of a burden to have five or six bright, motivated individuals working for you. But there are two problems:

1. If you're a growing business, you're going to need 25 employees, or 300, or 2,000, not just five—and not all of them are going to be as motivated as you would like.

2. No matter how loyal and talented your employees, as a company grows and diversifies, there inevitably comes a moment when you realize it takes more to create a team than team spirit.

## ORGANIZATIONAL STRUCTURE

In this chapter we're going to discuss how to create the infrastructure that will enable a small company to become a big one. Part of that process involves making smart hires and motivating employees, but we're going to save these topics for a later chapter because before we can talk about individuals, we have to talk about the organizational structure into which they will fit.

For most people, the words "organizational structure" bring to mind a chart in the classic pyramid shape with the CEO at the top and little boxes spread out in orderly rows below. This kind of chart may still accurately reflect the organization of many mature corporate giants, but it has little to do with the structure of a small start-up. Frankly, it's hard to find a start-up that even *has* an organizational chart.

Young entrepreneurial companies are characterized by a flexible, "do what it takes" atmosphere, loosely defined responsibilities, and a chronic shortage of staplers and paper clips. And as we've said before, this is exactly as it should be. Without a looseness of structure, a start-up would never be able to seize new opportunities, adapt rapidly to a shifting marketplace, or survive the shortages of capital that plague any new business.

However, if a company is going to avoid eventually hitting the wall, it will need to build a management team around some kind of a structure. The question is, what kind? Some entrepreneurs see this as an all-or-nothing proposition—freewheeling chaos or a rigid bureaucracy. Remember Larry Jones and his consumer electronics company, LJ Electronics? After the third-quarter loss of $6 million, Larry didn't have to be convinced that he needed more infrastructure. But as we discussed it with him, it became clear that his only notion of what infrastructure meant was a buttoned-down sort of organization with executive washrooms and layer after layer of middle management. Instinctively, he knew this was wrong for his business.

But acknowledging the need for infrastructure does not mean that you have to become a junior General Motors. These days, even large corporations are learning to install a flat rather than a deep management structure, with more independence of action asked of its managers and a faster response to new opportunities and risks.

A better organizational plan for LJ Electronics, or any small-to-midsized company, combines the flexible can-do atmosphere of a start-up with some of the accountability and control that is built into a more mature corporation. An organizational structure is useful only insofar as it helps to ensure that the company achieves its goals and objectives efficiently. A company can commission organizational charts that look beautiful on paper, but if they don't actively encourage a business to function at peak efficiency, then all that has been accomplished is to shuffle the chairs around. Thus, the best organizational structure is consistent with how work really gets done.

There are three basic ways to organize a business: functional, process, and matrix.

## The Functional Organization

A functional structure is the classical way businesses have organized themselves. For example, suppose you're a lamp-manufacturing company. To organize your company around functions, you'd break it down into its various logical functional components: manufacturing, materials, engineering, sales and marketing, human resources, and accounting and finance. As demand for your product increases, you simply add more people to each division as needed.

There are many advantages to this type of organization, not the least of which is its easy-to-understand logic. After all, these are, roughly speaking, the basic functional components of *every* business, so the system transplants well to almost any situation. A functional organizational structure also makes it easy to see who is responsible for what; there are few gray areas. If you need something manufactured, you know just which department to go to to get it done; if you need something sold or marketed, you know just who to see.

Of course, in the early stages of most entrepreneurial companies, many of these "departments" are all rolled into one. In some cases, they may all be rolled into a single person—you, the entrepreneur. But as the business grows, perhaps you hire someone to take over the hiring; you hire someone else to do the billing; you hire a manager to supervise manufacturing—and without even intending it, you have created a functionally organized company.

This is often how the organizational structure of a start-up evolves.

A functional structure works extremely well when you're a small company with a single product being sold in a single market. It begins to break down when you start to expand and diversify. Let's say your lamp manufacturing company, which began by making table lamps for the home, branches out into surgical operating-room lamps as well. So now you have two products, being sold in two quite different markets.

Your single sales department now has to talk to two entirely different kinds of customers: on the one hand, hospitals and medical supply houses; on the other, stores and home-appliance suppliers. Instead of building relationships with one type of customer in one market, the sales department must try to do the same with two sets of customers in different markets. Let's suppose your sales staff is successful and takes a large number of orders for the two different kinds of lamps. Now manufacturing has to *produce* both kinds of lamps, with all the added logistics that implies—and the inherent conflicts that emerge when bottlenecks develop. A large order for one type of lamps could easily delay a small order for the other type, which could damage your relationship with a customer. Meanwhile, the materials department, which must supply the raw products out of which the lamps are constructed, has to keep enough materials in inventory to produce *both* types of lamps, and accounting must work with materials to decide how much of which kind of inventory they can afford to buy and in what quantity.

With the rapid changes that take place in today's market, a company that does not diversify risks annihilation. And yet, with each new product, and each new market, a functionally organized company becomes ever more unwieldy.

Our lamp company was hypothetical. Let's take a real example: Sanders Parts, Inc., a Midwestern auto-parts manufacturer. Like many auto-part manufacturers, Sanders supplied several different major American car companies, and a couple of foreign-owned car companies as well. Sanders Parts had been around since the time of Henry Ford. It was well established and—because its contracts were based on long-standing relationships—pretty stable.

The management team was organized around a traditional functional structure according to Exhibit 3-1:

This structure, implemented at the very beginning of the company's existence, had worked extremely well for a long time. But in 1992, when they called us in, it was beginning to fray around the edges.

The company had three major customers, and from these customers' perspective, the situation was far from ideal. For one thing, the customers were continually getting bombarded with phone calls. Every department of Sanders Parts seemed to need to talk to them. The calls from the sales force were to be expected. Unfortunately, the sales people often didn't have the manufacturing information the

**Exhibit 3-1**
Management Team—Traditional Functional Structure

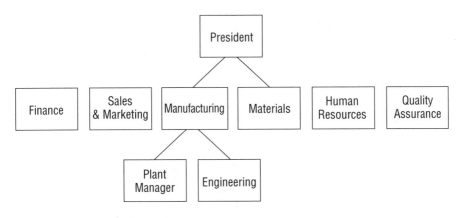

customers needed, so manufacturing called to tell the customers about delivery schedules and to get specifications. Accounts receivable, quality assurance, materials—all of these departments seemed to need to talk to the customers.

For another thing—at least from the customers' perspective—these different departments of Sanders Parts didn't seem to be talking to *each other* very much. A representative from Ford could give his sales contact at Sanders an important piece of information, and then two weeks later be obliged to repeat it to someone in accounts receivable.

The customers' trade secrets were also being compromised. In many cases, Sanders was producing the parts for rival companies on the same factory floor, where inquisitive eyes from one customer could glean details of another's new line.

And most important of all, a big order from one customer continually threatened the delivery schedules for the others. Because there were only a small number of manufacturing plants, it was physically impossible to meet peak demand.

Of course, all these situations had existed for some time, but several factors were beginning to make them more troublesome for Sanders' customers. Competition from overseas had created the need for a much more streamlined process, with faster turnaround times and more reliable deadlines. And, as the major car companies themselves were being forced to pay more attention to their customers' needs, they began to expect a higher level of service themselves from their subcontractors.

The general unhappiness was not confined to Sanders' customers. Within Sanders Parts itself there was also a widespread feeling of dissatisfaction. The salespeople were trying to cultivate three rival companies, and as a consequence, continually felt their loyalties being questioned and tested. Manufacturing had to keep track of three very different ordering systems, sets of specifications, and quality-control systems. Finance had to keep track of three different billing systems, three different fiscal years, and somehow continue the juggling act of allocating capital to different inventory stocks.

As a result of all these strains, Sanders Parts started missing its delivery dates. If a critical problem emerged, the company would mobilize to put out that fire, but in the process they would start another. When manufacturing fell behind on Ford parts, they would drop everything to finish the order, which meant they got behind on their Toyota orders.

All of this cost the company both in overtime and in goodwill. Finally, the management of Sanders decided something had to be done. Their first proposed solution was to lay off a lot of workers and retrench. But after some discussion, they decided instead to reorganize the company around its processes.

## The Process Organization

When a company organizes around critical processes, it is trying to implement a structure that mimics how the company actually does business. How a company does business is defined by the critical business processes it uses to meet customer needs. These processes include customer relationships, order fulfillment, and customer support. Typically, the company is broken down into a number of strategic business units—divisions of the company that are based not on function, but on critical processes.

For example, a company could organize its processes around product lines. That hypothetical lamp company we were discussing earlier could be split into two business units: one to take care of its table lamps, the other to handle the hospital lamps. Each of its units would include all the key personnel involved in the making of *that one product*, from sales and marketing people to manufacturing people to back-office finance people.

Or a company could organize its processes around its different markets. For example, the lamp company could again organize itself into two slightly different business units, one based on the consumer market, one based on the industrial market. Functionally, this might seem the same with only the two types of lamps the company now produces. But organizing around markets might bring a real advantage if the company were going to diversify into other products handled by the same buyers.

A company could also organize its processes around geographic markets. The Thompson Company, whose strategic plan we talked about in the last chapter, based one of its strategic business units on a geographic location rather than on a specific product.

Finally, a company could organize its processes around its major customers. This was the way Sanders Parts decided to go. After a strategic planning session similar to the one we described in the last chapter, Sanders reorganized according to Exhibit 3-2. Each of the first three strategic business units was responsible for servicing one—and only one—customer.

For example, the GM strategic business unit dealt exclusively with every aspect of Sanders' work for General Motors. Within the SBU were all the people who dealt with that customer or the customer's products. Each unit had three managers—a customer-contact process manager, a support-services process manager, and an order-fulfillment process manager. Anyone who had any contact with the customer, from sales and marketing to liaison people inside the plant, all reported through the customer-contact process manager. This en-

**Exhibit 3-2**
Reorganization of Strategic Business Units

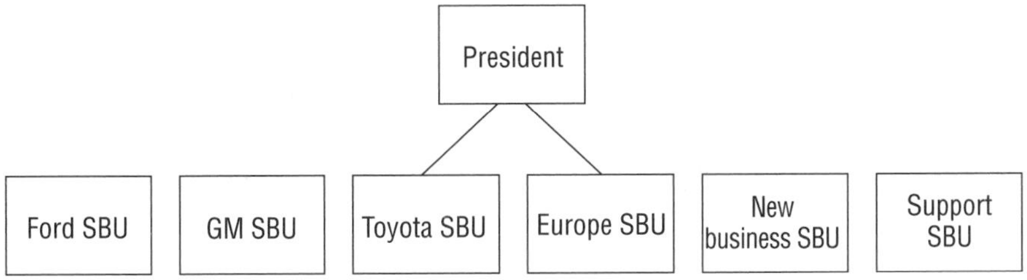

sured that the customer was always dealing with the same person, and that manager could really get to know what the customer wanted. The order-fulfillment manager was in charge of every aspect of taking in raw material, manufacturing it into finished parts, and delivering it to the customer. The support-services process manager took care of accounting, billing, human resources, and quality-support issues.

To ensure that there were no production logjams, and to eliminate divided loyalties, Sanders' factories were split up so that each of the client-based SBUs had its own factory with its own personnel.

Sanders recognized that the future depended on new business, so it formed the Europe and New Business SBUs. In time, each could spawn new SBUs devoted to single clients if demand justified it. The support SBU included overall financial, accounting, and human resources departments for the company.

The advantages of switching to a process structure were easy to see in Sanders' case. By focusing on their primary customers, they ensured that these customers would remain loyal. By putting all the processes pertaining to a single customer into the same strategic business unit, they ensured responsibility and accountability on the part of the employees. And by making each team responsible for only one customer, they helped to build a sense of loyalty and team spirit.

In the end, no employees were laid off. In fact, Sanders Parts ended up hiring *more* people. And instead of retrenching and losing money, the company posted record profits and record sales within a year of its reorganization.

From a pure theory viewpoint, the best part of all this was the elegance of the solution. During phase three of their strategic planning, the management of Sanders decided their most important goal was to satisfy their primary customers. The organization they created perfectly mirrored that goal.

## The Matrix Organization

A matrix organization is a combination of elements of a functional organization and a program/product or project organization. We see these organizations develop when an additional level of control is required, or as a reaction or overreaction to past problems such as quality or delivery.

Matrix organizations are characterized by redundant functions, empire building, and multiple reporting responsibilities. For example, a matrix organization might have a traditional engineering functional organization and also have the same and/or different engineers housed in a product-centered group. These engineers would, in essence, be serving two masters: the functional head (the director of engineering) and also the product manager. Matrix organizations can always be identified by a lot of "dotted line" reporting.

Many defense-related companies both large and small have embraced matrix organizations as a way to monitor performance of government contracts. A good example of a matrix organization is illustrated by Exhibit 3-3, depicting the management reporting structure of a company we will call Lancor. This company had both a functional organization and a program/product organization. In addition, employees were also organized by the buildings where they happened to work.

As you can tell by this mapping of the actual reporting structure, everyone in the organization was serving multiple masters. This

**Exhibit 3-3**
Existing Management Reporting Structure

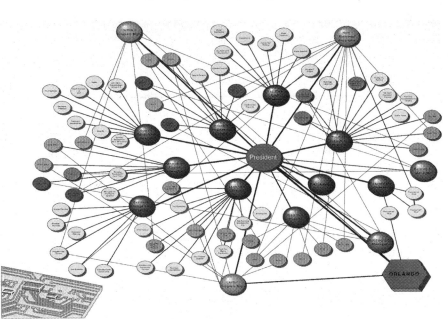

caused a lot of turmoil in the organization and also contributed to losses of productivity and excess cost. Effective communication was a constant challenge for this organization. Decisions had to be made by very large groups of constituents. Individual employees were often confused and frustrated.

Lancor's management came to us with a big challenge. They wanted to diversify away from defense-related business to more commercial business. They wanted to leverage their defense-related technology and find commercial applications. Could they actually be competitive in the commercial world?

We told them they would have an uphill battle. There were many areas in which they'd be at a competitive disadvantage to commercial companies—not the least of which was their matrix organization. Most world-class commercial companies are not saddled with this kind of bloated organization. Besides being noncompetitive from a cost standpoint, their organization was not flexible enough to react quickly to decisions that had to be made in the normal course of commercial business.

The Lancor management knew they had to simplify. With our help, they redesigned their organization. The resulting reporting structure is presented in Exhibit 3-4.

By contrast to the original organization, reporting structures have been simplified, spans of control have been reduced, and empires have been dissolved. No longer is the organization a multidimensional matrix. Product/program and building dimensions have been removed. The organization was designed around the critical processes and functions it performs. It became much more flexible and responsive. The organization required a lot fewer managers to perform effectively. Lancor's competitive cost position improved. Although the company is still in the defense business today, they have diversified into several commercial ventures. With a leaner, less complicated organization, they are well positioned to compete effectively in the future.

## WHEN IS IT TIME TO REORGANIZE?

Clients are always asking us for a dollar figure. "Should we reorganize at $10 million? Can we wait until we hit $20 million?" We've

**Exhibit 3-4**
Proposed Management Reporting Structure

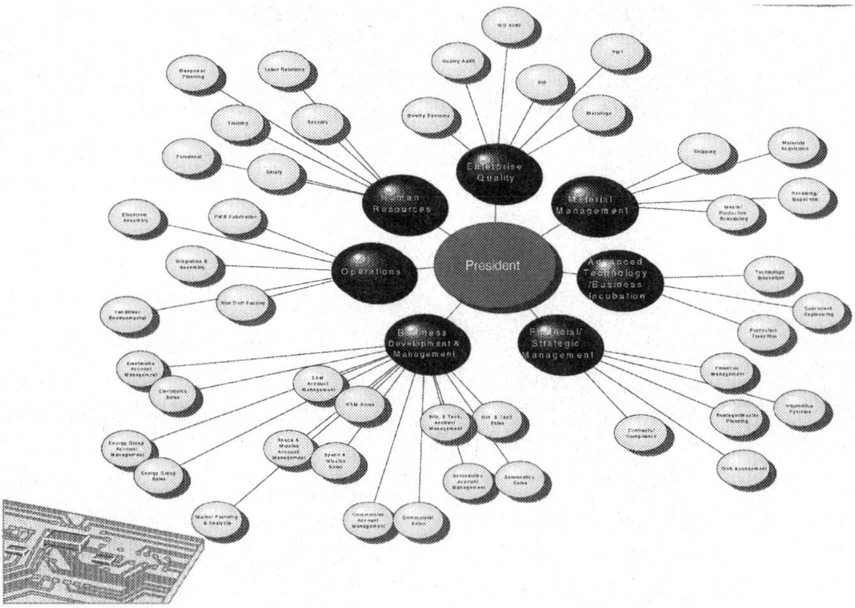

found it is difficult to use earnings as a reliable yardstick. The nature of some businesses allows them to muddle along without much infrastructure well past the $30 million mark, when other businesses would already be in trouble at $5 million.

However, there are three pretty reliable indicators. It's time to think about restructuring as soon as you start to see fiefdoms emerge. It's time to restructure when different divisions start hoarding information. And it's time to restructure when you begin to see turf wars break out. These are the early signs that your organizational structure is no longer efficient.

These problems can all be fixed by organizing around critical processes. For example, a company organized around teams each devoted to a single process will have little place for individuals who are not team players. Personal fiefdoms tend only to flower in function-oriented companies.

A process-structured company also finds ways to eliminate many of the personal advantages a manager might enjoy through withholding information from colleagues. As a member of a team organized around a single process, that manager has every reason to ensure that his team has all pertinent information.

## STRUCTURE IS ALWAYS EVOLVING

No matter which organizational structure you choose for your company, you can be sure of one thing: It won't look exactly the same in five years. As a company evolves and grows, its organizational needs change.

This will happen because businesses today are customer-driven—and the customer wants flexibility and responsiveness. Just keeping the customer happy will force you to modify your organization.

Another reason for change has become known as the Hawthorne effect. Way back in 1927, a Harvard Business School professor named Elton Mayo did a study based on workers in a Western Electric company at the Hawthorne Works in Illinois. For five years, he studied five women workers who were assembling relay units. The study was designed to see how working conditions affected productivity.

Mayo changed the group's wage incentives, and productivity went up. He changed the lighting and ventilation, and productivity went up again. He changed the number of hours the women worked in a row, and productivity went up. Finally, with the study complete, working conditions reverted back to the way they had been before the study.

And productivity went up again. At first, no one could understand what had happened. But it turned out that the individual changes Mayo made to working conditions were less important than the fact that the conditions were being changed. Over the years of the study, these five women had bonded into a team. They were aware that they were part of an important study, and the fact that their working conditions were being changed every once in a while just made life more interesting. So naturally, productivity went up with each change—even the change back to the way things had been before.

Change just for the sake of change is a valuable stimulus in business, at *every* level of the organization. And it's because of the constant need for change on an individual level that jobs should not be defined too narrowly.

## ROLES RATHER THAN JOBS

In the old days, a job description spelled out the minute details of an employee's day. It specified all the tasks and duties he was responsible for. It detailed who he was supposed to report to and who was under his supervision.

However, in today's fast-changing environment, detailed job descriptions have become outmoded. Twenty years ago, a person who was hired to publish promotional materials had a set of specific tasks to do that probably included spell-checking by hand, hiring linotype operators, and supervising the printing off-site. Today, with the advent of desktop publishing, most of these tasks have become obsolete. A traditional job description—even if it was written last week—would not give this employee the latitude to explore some new technology that will undoubtedly be available next month.

Instead of job descriptions, the modern company should outline roles. Roles helps people understand who is responsible for accomplishing what—but only in the most general terms. At their most basic level, roles define and explain why a position is necessary in a company, what contribution is expected, and how each position relates to others in the organization.

A role description defines responsibilities in terms of the core elements of the long-term strategy of the organization, but it does so with enough flexibility that the employee can respond to important changes in the direction and goals of the organization. It should not detail specifically how people will accomplish their responsibilities or even how their accomplishments will be measured—that's better left to annual performance planning—but it should clarify how work gets accomplished and how customers are served. Roles sometimes get defined in terms of "competencies" and "work processes."

We aren't big fans of jargon, but these two seem useful. Competencies are the skills, knowledge, and abilities required to fulfill a role and achieve organizational goals and objectives. Competencies could be specific task-related technical skills or interpersonal working skills. Both types of competencies are critical to fulfilling most organizational goals.

Work processes are the functions, operations, actions, or changes necessary to produce a result, a product, or a service. These may be accomplished by individuals or by teams, manually or with the use of technology.

Role descriptions shouldn't be limited just to management positions; they're useful for the rank and file as well. Let's take a person whose job it is to punch holes. If his job description only specified that he has to punch holes, then he won't necessarily know that he's responsible for the total quality effort of the product while it's under his care. He won't know that he is as responsible for its delivery to the customer as the man who transports it in his truck.

Involve the worker in the big picture, and everything changes. If he knows the reason *why* he's doing this work, he'll make intelligent decisions on the job—and if he's truly feeling empowered, he might just come up to his boss and say, "You know, I can do this better and faster if you would let me punch the metal sheets three at a time."

## ESTABLISHING BOUNDARIES . . .

A good role description establishes boundaries as well. Boundaries help individuals and work teams to focus on their primary responsibilities—the tasks no one else is going to accomplish.

Remember Charles Travis, of Travis Housewares? One of the hardest habits he had to break was micromanaging his employees. Since the company had no formal job descriptions (let alone role descriptions), he had formerly felt free to pull people off one project and put them on another, more or less at whim. This left many projects half-completed and many employees feeling frustrated and out of control.

When Travis Housewares started to define its employees roles in writing, Charles Travis was forced to change his behavior. When he went up to an employee and said, "You know what? Forget about doing the month-end analysis. I need you to do something else," the employee generally did what he had asked. But then the CFO (yes, we finally talked Charles into it) was able to say, "You know, Charles, we pay this guy a lot of money to do financial analysis. That's what he's good at, and that's what he's supposed to do."

## . . . BUT NOT AT THE EXPENSE OF CONTROL

Even in these days of team environments, organizational structure can, and should, include such traditional hierarchy-based concepts as "reporting relationships" and "span of control." These concepts are no longer trendy in business school models, but the notion of having a boss to whom you report, and who gives you supervision and guidance, is not all bad. In fact, it's pretty good. With the increasing use of telecommuting and on-site customer service, it's even more important for employees to feel a sense of belonging and to know how they fit into the big picture.

## HOW TO BUILD A TEAM

For a team to function well, an understanding of that big picture is vital. The company needs to clarify the team's purpose and strategic intent. What are its short and long-term goals? How will the team be measured and evaluated? When they're done, what will we see? What value will have been created?

Only when these questions have been answered will the team be able to do its job.

Of course, not only do you have to define what the team is going to do for you, but you also have to figure out what you have to give the team.

### Information

Perhaps the key thing an employer must give his team is information. Making information available to your employees sends a lot of messages: It says that you have trust and confidence in their discretion and abilities; it is a tacit encouragement for out-of-the-box thinking and innovations; it helps develop understanding when management has to make tough choices; and it allows the team to make intelligent decisions that you will be able to live with down the road.

This was a lesson that Katherine Briggs of House Fashion learned the hard way. You may remember that this brilliant salesperson had started a very successful women's clothing business about ten years before we met her. She'd even organized it well, with separate divisions for each product line and vice presidents in charge of each division. But Katherine hated to share information. She could never really explain why. Perhaps it was because she felt that as CEO and founder, only she was entitled to know the big picture. Perhaps she didn't really trust her managers. And perhaps it was because, subconsciously, she knew her bottom line was in trouble, and she didn't want anyone to confirm it for her. House Fashion's obsession with sales led it to wildly overspend on overhead, product design, and customer support—all of which eventually led to the banks trying to take over the business.

Interestingly enough, as Katherine tried to stave off the banks, she was forced to tell her managers what was happening. The managers finally got to see the bottom line—and with a gratifying alacrity they immediately began reigning in production costs. They also changed the incentive program for their salespeople from bonuses based simply on total sales to a more complicated system that incorporated the company's profitability.

For Katherine, all this was a revelation. Of course she knew *intellectually* that giving her employees information might help them to make better decisions, but seeing her managers working to save her company was when she finally got it.

## Guidance, Coaching, Training, and Development

Even the most sophisticated teams need leadership and assistance—and it's the company's job to provide both. A team must be accountable for its work, with goals worked out in advance. This means that for every team performing a task, there should be someone reviewing the work and providing feedback, assistance, and resources. But more important, someone outside the team needs to *care* about the team members' success. This person should be willing to run interference for the team when necessary. A team that doesn't feel its supervisor is willing to go to the mat for them will never be as devoted to the success of their project.

Part of the assistance a company can provide is training. Technologies change so quickly these days that the acquisition of additional technical skills is vital—but team members may need training in more basic skills as well. Elementary problem solving, decision making, and conflict resolution are all necessary in today's workplace. Until a few years ago, the average executive worked highly independently. Nowadays, to meet the complex challenges businesses face, people increasingly need to work together to accomplish goals or solve complex problems. This requires a high level of interaction—and this is a skill that is not routinely taught in school.

Part of the assistance a company can provide is instructional. An employer we know once took his top managers to a casino during one of the evenings of a strategic planning retreat. He split the executives into four teams, gave them each $1000, and told them they had one hour to go invest his money. They were all supposed to meet back at the conference room to report on their progress. It was fascinating to observe the risk aversion of some of the groups. One team simply held the money; they returned it to the CEO intact. Another went to the smoke shop and bought cigarettes to resell later at a profit (this was a Native American reservation casino where the cigarettes are sold tax-free). One group won a small amount. One group lost the entire $1,000.

The CEO listened to the teams' reports and then said, "Listen. Every day, in the course of business, you go out and risk my money. It may not feel that way, but every decision you make is an educated bet. And I just hope you will be as careful and thoughtful with my money Monday through Friday as you have been tonight."

## Keeping Score

The final thing a company must provide for its teams is a yardstick. We all have a sense (for better or worse) of how we're doing at work. Sometimes our feelings are based on quantifiable evidence; sometimes they're completely subjective. Without actual measures, it's difficult to assess our own performance.

Measures have a couple of purposes. They help you understand how your team is doing, but more importantly, they give your team a way to gauge their own performance and progress—which will help them make adjustments and develop pride in their results.

Rewards may be, and often are, financial. But they don't always need to be. Your team wants to do well and succeed. They may be motivated by the promise of financial reward. But this does not mean they don't need intrinsic rewards as well. They want to know you know they're doing well and they want to hear you acknowledge it.

This can be accomplished through feedback and thanks, or through small tokens of appreciation. Intrinsic reward and heartfelt thanks can carry a team through difficult times (and even a small slump). We will detail all of this in our chapter on "Finding and Retaining Good People."

## DECIDING WHEN TO IGNORE CONSENSUS

Empowered employees. Self-directed teams. Consensus. These are the buzzwords right now, and with good reason. The concepts behind these words are the backbone of modern business. But sometimes it can all be overkill.

It is neither necessary nor healthy for every employee to be involved in every decision. We saw a small example of this recently, when the president of a company held a meeting with all his managers to talk about future goals. He wanted to empower his team, so he gave each of them three votes, and promised to abide by their decisions. So all 40 managers (some quite senior, but others only a few years out of college) got to vote on the future of the company. The junior managers had just as many votes as the senior managers.

When the votes were tabulated, the president was horrified. He had committed himself to a course of action that he realized only too late was not the way either he or his top executives wanted to go.

After some soul searching, he was forced to overrule the vote. A better way to proceed would have been to gather *information* from all 40 managers, and then get together with his senior staff to decide what to do.

## INFRASTRUCTURE

Whether you are dealing with the structuring of an entire organization, a team, or an individual's role within that organization, there is always one basic concept to keep in mind: businesses today are customer-driven and customer-focused—and those customers demand flexibility and responsiveness. To provide these things, an entrepreneur must find ways to make her organizational structures flatter and more responsive to new opportunities and risks. Of course, these tasks are not mandatory for a company—as long as you don't mind staying at the same size you already are.

## ENTREPRENEUR'S SUMMARY

To avoid eventually hitting the wall, an expanding company will need to build a management team around some kind of a structure—and the best structure for young entrepreneurial companies incorporates the flexible can-do atmosphere of a start-up with some of the accountability and control that is built into a more mature corporation. However, an organizational structure is useful only insofar as it helps to ensure that the company achieve its goals and objectives efficiently.

There are three basic ways to organize a business:

1. A *functional organization* structures itself around functions, such as manufacturing, materials, engineering, sales and marketing, human resources, and accounting and finance. This is the simplest and most traditional structure, and works best when a company is selling a single product in a single marketplace.

2. In the *process organization*, a company organizes around critical processes. The critical processes it uses to meet customer needs include new-product development, order fulfillment, and customer support. Typically, a process-structured company is organized around one of three critical dimensions: product lines, markets, or major customers.

3. The *matrix organization* combines functional elements and product/market/customer structures. Typically, the functional divisions (human resources, operations, and engineering) are separate from process divisions dedicated to individual product lines, markets, or customers.

In our view, it makes the most sense for entrepreneurial companies to organize around processes. A good sign that it's time to do so is when fiefdoms and turf wars start to emerge.

Process-driven structures need to be flexible because businesses today are customer-driven—and the customer wants flexibility and responsiveness. Keeping the customer happy will force you to modify your organization continually.

In order to be effective, a process-driven company needs to provide five things for its employees:

1. *Role descriptions* to let the employee know what he is responsible for accomplishing. In today's fast-changing business climate, roles should not be defined too narrowly.

2. *Reporting relationships,* which detail to whom the employee reports and delineate who will provide him with guidance and supervision.

3. *Information* to enable the employees to understand their goals and to show them you have trust in their discretion and abilities.

4. *Leadership* to provide feedback, assistance, resources, training to keep up with process improvement, and the all-important sense that what the team is doing matters.

5. *Objective measures of performance and goals.*

# Developing a Management Information Reporting System

Frank Murphy should have been a happy man. Frank had started his specialty footwear business with a simple, brilliant idea: making comfortable shoes in extra-wide and extra-narrow sizes. The result: Wide and Narrow Shoes had five factories, revenues of $150 million, and orders flooding in daily. It seemed like everyone in the country with an odd-size foot wanted a pair of Frank's shoes. The joke around the office was that if everyone with an odd-size foot bought a pair of Frank's shoes, podiatrists all over the country would go out of business. But Frank was not amused.

There was something drastically wrong with inventory and Frank couldn't figure it out. Management reports indicated one set of numbers for how much raw material and finished-goods inventories were on hand, but every time a physical inventory was taken, the numbers failed to match. As an experienced manufacturer, Frank knew how dangerous inventory discrepancies could be. If a company doesn't know how much inventory it has, it can miss sales opportunities due to stock outs; it can't really tell how much its products cost; and it won't know—in an overall sense—how the business is doing. And the discrepancies in question were huge, representing millions of dollars worth of product.

Why didn't the figures tally? Was somebody stealing? Was management covering up? How could Frank run a $150 million company without knowing his bottom line? He'd borrowed heavily from the banks. What was he supposed to tell them? They'd seen the reports and were calling weekly. The company, seemingly a huge success, was in fact perched on the brink of collapse.

## INFORMATION SYSTEMS

When we were called in to Wide and Narrow Shoes, it didn't take long to identify the main cause of Frank's problem: His information system was inadequate—it couldn't tell him what his products cost. A good information system is one of the most important tools management has. It is no exaggeration to say that a good information system can save a business and a bad one can bankrupt it. Why? Because information is power.

By information system, we do not mean simply computer hardware and software. We mean the entire system of people, machines, and methods by which records of business transactions are developed, compared, distributed, analyzed, and acted upon.

At its simplest level, an information system is a checkbook. That, after all, is what an entrepreneur usually starts out with: a checkbook and a dream. In the very beginning, he might make two or three sales a day. He enters the cash receipts as deposits in his checkbook register, pays the bills—and the balance in his checkbook is his bottom line.

Of course, once the number of customers and sales increase, a checkbook becomes inadequate, and it's time to add a basic accounting system. Whether it exists as a series of handwritten books or as a software program, an accounting system is a record of basic information—for example, sales broken down by customer (and even this simple piece of data can give the entrepreneur valuable information). The information contained in an accounting system is an entrepreneur's guide to his customers' preferences, spending habits, and credit problems—if he's willing to look at it.

Naturally, no one builds a successful business without looking at *some* information. Believe us, *every* entrepreneur we've met looks at cash in the bank, sales figures, how many orders the company's shipped, and how many people are in the field (if it's a sales organization) or hours billed (if it's a service business). But there's a world of information beyond these simple numbers that can be critical to building your business.

For the sake of simplicity, let's say you own a company that manufactures a line of women's clothing, and one of your customers is the Betty's Boutique chain. Your accounting reports will list all the invoices you've sent to Betty's. And in looking over those invoices, you might notice that the boutique paid its bill for October, but not for September. Well, why not? Did they not get the bill? Or did they perhaps disagree with the charges, but forgot to call you about it? Keeping your customers satisfied is even more critical in today's business environment than it ever was, and your accounting reports can be a valuable tool if you really look at them. Perhaps the missing payment is an early indication that Betty's Boutique is experiencing a cash-flow problem; if you were counting on Betty's for its monthly miniskirt order, you might want to make a cautious phone call.

The point is that you can use your information system to look for patterns. Sales have been going down for the past four months; what does that mean? Sales of skirts are going up while sales of dresses are down; if you learn this in time, you might manufacture more skirts and fewer dresses.

Once your business reaches a certain size, you simply cannot be everywhere at once. Having accurate information to look at will tell you where to concentrate your attention. The information is both a surrogate for your presence and an early-warning system.

All these things can be accomplished from a basic accounting system. But now imagine that your accounting system could also somehow:

- Keep track of your company's multiple locations and products, with all relevant information arriving neatly broken down into useful categories, on a computer screen each morning.

- Tell you at a glance exactly what your profit margin is at any moment on any item you produce.

- Tell you at a glance exactly what your profit margin *would be* if you opened a new factory or closed an old factory, hired or fired personnel, or changed your manufacturing process.

- Indicate *exactly* how much inventory you need— eliminating the need to keep vital capital tied up in excess safety-inventory stocks.

Imagine that your accounting system could get you all this information in a timely manner so that you knew what was happening in your market before your competitors did.

Imagine that it had safeguards built into it so that it could detect inaccuracies in data-entry, detect the possibility of fraud, and detect expensive tax-calculation mistakes.

Imagine that it could look into the future and create a budget for the next year, and at the press of a button allow you to compare your actual performance against that projected budget and even against the performance of your competitors.

All this is what a good information system can do for you.

As your company grows beyond the capacities of a basic accounting system and a part-time accountant, you need to know at a glance what your income and expenses are. You need a full management information system that will provide the detail you need—by customer, product line, market, and business unit or territory. You need to keep track of inventory, allocate costs, budget realistically, and benchmark. You need to generate reports with performance measures as well as key financial statistics such as profitability ratios, turnover ratios, leverage ratios, and return on investment. And beyond all that, you need an early-warning system to tell you when your business is in trouble.

In this chapter, we're not going to tell you everything there is to know about management information systems. Nor are we going to explain in detail the minutiae of accounting. But we *are* going to tell you:

- The underlying principles behind a good system: accuracy and timeliness.

- The areas in which mistakes are most commonly made: narrowly focusing on only some numbers, allocating costs incorrectly, and failing to keep track of inventory.

- The kinds of practices that will help you take your company into the future: budgeting, the use of performance measures, and some straightforward reporting techniques such as flash reporting and the use of roll-forwards. Exhibit 4-1 provides an overview of an ideal reporting hierarchy. Based on these reporting tools, a senior executive will have all of the pertinent information needed to keep a pulse on the business.

## Accuracy

The first principle of an information system is accuracy. Information doesn't do you any good if it's not reliable. This may seem obvious, but you'd be surprised at how much faulty data plagues even large, successful companies.

Often, the reason is multiple inputting. It's one of the most common problems we see. Typically, what happens is something like this: A customer calls up and places an order into the customer-service system; then the order is reentered into the manufacturing system. Unfortunately, the manufacturing system doesn't generate invoices from orders, so the information has to be reentered into a separate accounting system for an invoice to be generated. That's three entries—so far—of the same information.

After this many entries, the chances that it's the same information have diminished drastically—and once the information is in the system inaccurately, it leads to further errors: you make decisions based on erroneous information; you bill customers incorrectly; you don't collect the right amounts of money; you don't follow up on old receivables promptly enough; or you duplicate bills and anger customers. One mistake leads to more mistakes.

Another way inaccuracies creep into the system is when offices or individual employees keep a set of their own records, which aren't linked to the main records of the company. One area where this is common is sales, where salespeople keep their own records in order to calculate their commissions. It also happens when managers get frustrated because their company's information system is incapable of giving them the data they need. In either case, after a while there are two parallel systems with two different sets of numbers, and no one is entirely sure which is correct. Inconsistent reporting can lead to big mistakes because the company ends up using numbers a salesperson jotted down on the back of an envelope. Those numbers may then get into the salesperson's computer and never filter into the

**Exhibit 4-1**
Contents of a Comprehensive Management Report

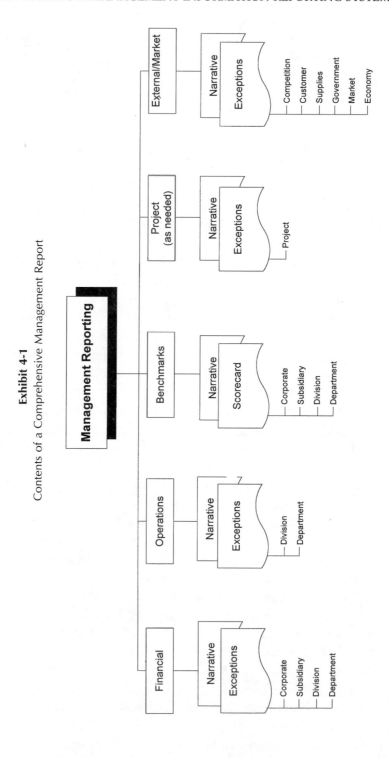

company system, where they might be reconciled. Or worse, they *do* get into the company's system and taint it.

The ideal way to avoid both these problems—multiple inputting and inconsistent reporting—is to get a fully integrated computerized system. In this kind of system, information gets entered once and is accessible for various kinds of processing from a central database.

The more sophisticated integrated information systems can create a budget and compare it to your actual results and/or the previous period or year, enable you to revise your budget based on more current figures, and give you a quick glance at a set of key performance measures and statistics for specified periods of time. Most sophisticated systems will enable you to manage all factories and product lines. And many support vendor-managed inventory—a process in which your computer can look directly into your customer's computer and automatically determine when your customer needs new stock from you.

Not every company can afford a state-of-the-art, fully integrated system like the ones we've just described. But there are literally thousands of systems out there with a wide range of prices and capabilities. Any good system should be able to do basic accounting: journals, ledgers, and weekly, monthly, and quarterly reports. This will enable you to generate financial statements, including a balance sheet and an income statement. When the basics are in the system, reports can then be produced that include key operating and management statistics, such as the number of units produced, inventory levels, employee head counts, aged accounts-receivable balances, measures of product profitability, etc.

Today, software products are tailored for your specific line of business—and many of these programs have general accounting systems built into them, or come as add-on modules to a basic accounting system. This specialized software exists for all kinds of businesses, from restaurant-supply companies to law firms. We'll talk more about the technical side of information systems in the next chapter, but a good resource for buying software is Datapro, a directory of software packages. Datapro will tell you what computers a particular kind of software runs on.

But whatever system and/or software you buy, the purchase is just the beginning. What counts is how you set it up, and then how you use it. Of course, when you switch to a more elaborate form of accounting, it is critical to develop a system of financial controls. See Appendix B for examples of controls and guidelines.

### Timeliness Is Next to Godliness

In order to be useful, information has to be not just accurate, but timely—and sometimes it's worth sacrificing a little accuracy for a lot of timeliness.

So that's what we advised Frank to do at Wide and Narrow.

There's an old concept called the Parreto Principle, which says that a few transactions will account for the vast majority of the result (and vice versa). This is just the principle that common sense has taught us: Some things are more important than others. In the case of Wide and Narrow Shoes, our study indicated that 10 categories of the 5,000 shoe materials made up 90% of the materials cost. And 10 items are a lot easier to track than 5,000.

Since they already knew their labor and overhead costs, we suggested that, on an interim basis, those 10 items be tracked (along with labor and overhead) using an inexpensive PC system. Frank also got his industrial engineering staff to adjust technical standards (estimates of how much leather, time, and effort goes into the making of a shoe), as experience showed the current standards were faulty. This worked so well that Frank was able to keep a handle on inventory for the next two years while a major integrated system was developed.

Timeliness is a particularly important value for manufacturing companies like Wide and Narrow because it allows them to spot slow-moving inventory. If trends can be spotted quickly enough, problems can be dealt with. For instance, if sales are going down, you can take action to anticipate the problem by slowing down production on the items that aren't selling, or you can stop production entirely on those items and husband your resources. At the very worst, you can stop throwing good money after bad—but only if you know that there's a problem early on.

The Parreto Principle also applies to customers. If your system can't give you information about all your customers fast enough, then at least look at your major customers; that will give you a pretty good sense of how business is.

Another good business practice for generating timely information is the use of flash reports. Flash reports are monthly or semi-monthly reports on key variables that give you a quick picture of your business by using estimates and assumptions about basic costs. What those key variables are will differ from one business to the next. For instance, in a law firm, the key numbers will be billable hours. In a manufacturing firm, they will more likely be gross sales and units produced. No matter what the business, a flash report gives you a fast educated guess about your bottom line. (See Exhibit 4-2).

Flash reports have to be looked at with a practiced eye. To take the example of a law firm again, if some of those billable hours represent pro bono work, then they shouldn't be counted. If a customer is unlikely ever to pay his bill, this money should not be treated as if it is in the bank. In effect, flash reports emphasize timeliness over accuracy. This trade-off is often worth it.

## Focus on the Whole Picture

A good information system gives you the ability to spot patterns—but you have to know what to look for. When a company is young and small, CEOs can often get "a sense of the business" by looking at sales and one or two other key numbers. But as the company grows, these rules of thumb stop working. If management doesn't start looking at the whole picture, it can be a recipe for disaster.

We saw just such a disaster narrowly averted recently at a company called Comp-U-Tech. Comp-U-Tech provides computer programmers on a temporary basis for businesses. It's a simple operation: little overhead, very little permanent staff, and no materials coming in. In fact, it's so simple that Comp-U-Tech had grown rapidly to annual revenues of $100 million dollars with a very rudimentary information system. They didn't even have a budget.

The CEO had a simple rule of thumb to tell how business was going. Every morning, he'd get a report with a count of how many people he had out in the field. The more people out in the field, the healthier his company. This worked quite well until the nature of the business started changing. Customers began asking for deals by project. Comp-U-Tech had previously charged per person per day; now, they were being asked to take on bigger projects and bid them at a flat fee.

**Exhibit 4-2**

Sample Flash Report for an Apparel Company

Net Sales

Gross Profit (%)

Inventory Turns

| | Month | | | | Year to Date | | | YTD Trend to Pin |
|---|---|---|---|---|---|---|---|---|
| | % Variance | | | | | % Variance | | ♦ Favorable |
| Key Indicators/Measures | LY | Plan | Actual | Actual | LY | Plan | | ◆ Unfavorable |
| Number of stores | 0 | 0 | 58 | 58 | 6 | 0 | – |
| **Sales Measures ($000)** | | | | | | | |
| Net Sales | 40% | 10% | $4,460 | $14,648 | 40% | 10% | ♦ |
| Markdowns | 42% | 3% | $795 | $2,834 | 33% | 3% | ◆ |
| Return on Sales | 4% | 7% | 16% | 16% | 1% | 6% | ♦ |
| Sale per Employee | 42% | 10% | $8,355 | $25,526 | 42% | 10% | ♦ |
| Sales per SKU | 15% | 10% | $166 | $463 | 8% | 7% | ♦ |
| **Income Measures** | | | | | | | |
| Gross Profit as % of Sales | 44.0% | 12.0% | 56.3% | 55.0% | 43.0% | 9.0% | ♦ |
| EBIT ($000) | 84% | 9% | $626 | $2,236 | 60% | 10% | ♦ |
| **Expense Measures** | | | | | | | |
| Occupancy Exp. as % of Sales | 18% | (10%) | 8% | 8% | 22% | (4%) | ♦ |
| Delivery Exp. % of Sales | 1% | 2% | 7% | 0% | 0% | 1% | ◆ |
| Sales Payroll as % of Sales | 56% | 34% | 4% | 4% | 56% | 34% | ◆ |
| G & A as % of Sales | 68% | (17%) | 5% | 4% | 62% | (14%) | ♦ |
| Home Office Exp. as % of Sales | 21% | (1%) | 10% | 9% | 28% | (10%) | ♦ |
| Travel and Entertainment | (79%) | 11% | $ 3,220 | $ 25,262 | 42% | 271% | ◆ |
| **Other Measures** | | | | | | | |
| Shrinkage as % of Sales | 1.0% | 1.0% | 1.59% | 1.60% | (2.0%) | (2.0%) | ♦ |
| Inventory Turns | (0.1) trns | 0.1 trns | 1.2 | 1.4 | (0.1) trns | 0.1 trns | ♦ |
| Sales Over/ Short | (83%) | (131%) | ($51) | $ 1,169 | 100% | 30% | ◆ |

This potentially allowed Comp-U-Tech to do larger jobs, make more money, and grow the company. The only problem was that the CEO was still measuring how his company was doing by looking at how many programmers were in the field. Recently, a large project proved to be more complicated than anticipated; it took 25 additional programmers and three extra weeks. Based on the "programmers in the field" formula, they were making even more of a profit. But actually, since the job had been contracted for a flat fee, the contract was losing a substantial amount of money.

This was Comp-U-Tech's wake-up call. Comp-U-Tech's managers realized they would need to develop a sophisticated method for costing out projects so that their bids on fixed-fee jobs would enable them to turn a profit. They also realized that now that the company was offering two different kinds of services, their whole management information system, and quite possibly their company infrastructure, were going to have to change.

Comp-U-Tech is typical of rapidly growing entrepreneurial companies: Its information system had lagged behind its growth. At Comp-U-Tech, the problem was caught in time; in too many cases it is not. The key is to change behavior. A wake-up call of some type forces management to look at the whole—not just at one or two indicators.

## Performance Measures

A classic example of the kind of crisis a company can get into when it outgrows its information system is Larry Jones's LJ Electronics, the consumer electronics company that we discussed in chapter one. The problem at LJ Electronics was that although sales were going up, deep discounts and volume rebates were wiping out profit margins. Larry *did* have an information system. The numbers were there if he'd gone looking for them, and you could say that most of his problems were of his own doing. But he wasn't helped by an information system that was rather rudimentary for a company of LJ Electronics's size. If LJ Electronics had had the kind of integrated system that could compare actual results with a budget, Larry would have seen in advance that his profit margins were declining and that soon every sale he was going to make would actually be *costing* him money.

A good information system will tell you what your profit margins are for any given item. This is critical not only to determining the pricing of your product and the health of your bottom line, but to issues of growth. Your company doesn't have to be in the straits LJ Electronics was for there to be a problem with profit margins. If your margins are low, that may be a signal that you need to change the focus of your business. (You may remember low profit margins proved to be the key to the stalled growth of the BL Thompson Company in chapter three.)

A good information system will also generate key financial statistics on profitability, productivity, and liquidity that are important both to you and your investors. These include sales volume and growth; profit margins; working capital and leverage measures; gross profit by customer, product, or service; return on sales; and return on net assets. These statistics tell you where there are problems and highlight where there are new opportunities. What it all boils down to is ROI: return on investment. Every top manager faces a continual set of decisions. Do I invest in a new product line? How much should I spend on R&D? Should I get rid of this losing division, or try to turn it around? These decisions all hinge on a complete set of factors that tell you what's currently happening in your business. If the numbers your system generates tell you that a new product line will only get you a 3% return on your investment, you might think twice and spend the money on something promising a higher rate of return.

This is not to say that every start-up business needs a system that generates sophisticated management statistics. In fact, for a small company, at an early stage where things are easy to keep track of and where all the energy is directed at staying afloat, a sophisticated system may be a burden and a mistake. The key is knowing when you've passed out of that stage and into the next. For, as a business grows, it inevitably changes. You can't go on relying on what used to work. As we've seen, customers change, markets change, price structures change; you can't rely on old assumptions. Especially not when it comes to that most critical of measures: what it costs you to make your product or deliver your service. (For a comprehensive set of performance measures by process area see Appendix C: New Metrics for a New Age)

## Cost Accounting

How much does it cost you to make your product? This is one of the most important pieces of information a businessperson needs to have. If you want to make money, the price of your product has to cover your costs. This may seem obvious, but many companies run aground because figuring out how much it costs to make a product or deliver a service can be complicated.

Cost allocation has traditionally been based on man-hours or machine-hours worked on a product. In traditional cost accounting, overhead costs (such as heating or engineering costs) would be allocated to a particular product based on the proportion of direct labor hours used to make that product. The problem with this cost-allocation method in today's environment is that labor has become a shrinking proportion of costs. Labor as a trigger for allocating other costs often no longer makes sense.

Cost allocation is as vital for service firms as it is for manufacturers. For example, in a law firm, overhead costs can be allocated to different departments (litigation, corporate, real estate, etc.) based on hours worked or gross revenue generated. But here too, this method doesn't take into account the cost of services actually used by each department.

To deal with this limitation, there is an increasingly popular method of cost allocation called "activity-based costing." Activity-based costing attempts to present as closely as possible how much any given item or activity costs. Let's return to our hypothetical lamp manufacturing company. Let's say the heating bill for your factory is $1,000 a month and you sell 1,000 lamps a month. It would seem to make sense to allocate the heating cost on the basis of one dollar per lamp. But what if some of the lamps you sell are imported, and all you do is put your label on them before shipping them to your customers? Why allocate part of the heating cost onto those lamps? The true cost of the imported lamps is lower. By understanding that, you can price those lamps lower—which may help to push up sales.

In another example, if your engineering department spent more time developing one lamp model than another, activity-based costing would allocate a bigger part of the engineering cost to that model, based on how much time the department really spent. Unless you know the true cost of making a product, you won't be able to price it fairly—and that represents an opportunity for your competition. If they're doing a better job of cost allocation than you are, they will be able to set better prices. And by better, we don't necessarily mean lower. A company that doesn't have an accurate idea of what it costs to make its product may set a price that is too low to provide a profit.

Accurate cost allocation is also crucial to bidding a job. Take the case of Mercury Science, a defense contractor, which didn't allocate costs properly. Mercury had spent almost $1 million developing two electronics systems. (In the interests of national security, let's call the two systems Product A and Product B.) They allocated costs equally to the two products, so on paper Product A cost half a million dollars to develop and Product B cost half a million dollars to develop. But in fact, the engineering department had spent 90% of its time on Product A and only 10% of its time on Product B. So Product A really cost $900,000 to develop, and Product B, $100,000.

It came time to bid the projects. Since the development costs had to be amortized over the sales life of the product, you'd have expected that Mercury would have asked for more money for Product A and less money for Product B. But they didn't.

They had allocated costs equally for both products, so they bid both products at the same price. Unfortunately for Mercury, their competition did not make this mistake. So Mercury won the bid for expensive Product A with a bid that was too low to profitably absorb development costs, and lost the bid for inexpensive Product B with a bid that was too high.

This wasn't the only bidding/cost-allocation problem Mercury had. They also had a problem getting their various departments to work together successfully.

Typically, the salespeople at Mercury would work with the engineering department to make up a successful bid. Engineering would put in all sorts of bells and whistles. Once they won the bid, the salespeople would go to manufacturing and show them the plans. The reaction of the folks at manufacturing? "We can't make this for what you budgeted! Where did you get these numbers!" In one case, the bid specified an expensive, hard to find, specially made part that could easily have been replaced with a much cheaper standard part from a hardware store. "What were you people thinking?" complained manufacturing.

Of course, what they were thinking was that they wanted to make the sale. Exacerbating the lack of communication between departments was the fact that the salespeople's bonuses were based on their sales, so their incentive was to make a sale, any sale, even if it wasn't profitable.

A good information system sets up procedures for pricing a new product that make it more difficult to ignore the actual costs of manufacturing. Just by having a few items devoted to cost allocation on its electronic form, a new-product software module will encourage a manager to consult with the people in engineering and the people in manufacturing. In the best of all possible worlds, different departments will voluntarily work together for a common goal. But in the real world, it doesn't hurt to have an information system that forces them to do so.

## Watch Your Inventory

If you're not allocating costs properly, one of the places problems are likely to show up is in inventory.

That, in fact, was what almost wrecked Frank Murphy's company, Wide and Narrow Shoes, the example that began this chapter. Frank called us because his estimated inventory never matched his physical inventory and the banks were breathing down his neck. Frank's accountants could keep track of labor and overhead, but tracking the materials defeated them. It was no wonder: It turned out there were 5,000 components that went into making Frank's different products. Using an antiquated information system, the accountants were overwhelmed by the details, trying to account for every last eyelet and piece of thread.

Compounding the problem were faulty estimates from the industrial engineering department. The company's engineers had underestimated the amount of labor and material that went into making the shoes. They'd also made faulty assumptions about how efficiently Frank's five different factories were operating. On paper, the factories were supposed to be producing $x$ number of shoes a day, using $x$ amount of material and labor. In real life, some workers at some factories were idle, waiting for materials to arrive, while other factories had material sitting around because the workers were very busy. The engineers had also made faulty assumptions about how many shoes could be made from one piece of leather. The amount of scrap material—pieces of leather, etc., that were too small to be of use—was much larger than anticipated. In other words, many of the assumptions that had gone into costing inventory were wrong. On top of all that, there was some pilferage.

Clearly, the ultimate solution was a fully integrated system, so the company could track the real costs. Frank planned to install a big, expensive system to do just that—but it would take two years to accomplish, and in two years, he could be out of business. Instead, he chose to develop a simplified, PC-based cost-accounting system which, as described earlier, tracked 90% of the cost of his materials. While he couldn't reconcile these reports with his general ledger, the numbers were close enough to enable him to run effectively until his new system was finished.

## Budgets

Up until now we've been talking about record-keeping as an enterprise that's historical ("What happened?") and topical ("What's happening right now?"). But a good information system will also enable you to plan for the future. That means looking forward and that means a budget.

A budget takes you into the future because it forces you to come up with a plan for the following year; instead of just responding to events, you're trying to guide them. It forces you and your entire organization to lay out goals and make choices about how to use your resources.

There are various methods of creating a budget, with differing degrees of sophistication. The simplest way to budget is to begin by looking at what you've spent in the past. If you're trying to come up with a number for the projected cost of heating your lamp factory, you could look at what you paid the previous year for that item. Then you figure in whatever costs you expect to be different: Perhaps you're going to be busier next year and will be spending more time in the factory, or perhaps the price of heating oil has changed. Often the way budgets get created is that a manager looks at last year's figures and adds five or ten percent. This is fast and convenient, but it's not always realistic.

**Exhibit 4-3**
Typical Steps in the Budget Process

| STEPS | TIMING |
|---|---|
| 1. Financial reporting package published with year-to-date amounts and projections through calendar year-end. Distributed to management of business units. | (Assume calendar fiscal year) Early October |
| 2. Executive prepares outline of goals for coming year and distributes to managers. | Early October |
| 3. Meeting of executive and managers is held to review plans and goals and to get feedback. | Mid-October |
| 4. Accounting distributes package of forms for managers to prepare budget for coming year. | End of October |
| 5. Managers prepare and submit forms to accounting which compiles preliminary overall budget. | Mid-November |
| 6. Executive reviews preliminary budget for reasonableness and to evaluate impact on fixed/overhead costs - (e.g., space, computer systems, insurance, etc.) | Late November |
| 7. Meetings are held with managers to refine assumptions and revise budget worksheets. Submit to accounting. | Early December |
| 8. Accounting prepares final budget, executive reviews and approval. Budget distributed to managers. | Mid-December |

A more accurate approach is zero-based budgeting, in which you go back to your basic requirements, without assuming anything. For instance, to budget your heating bill for next year, you'd look at your space, the number of BTUs needed, and how your usage compares to other usages. This method may be more time-consuming to set up initially, but once it's in place, it's relatively simple to plug in the numbers, and the more accurate results are often worth the effort. Inherent in this and other budgeting methodologies is the "build up" approach, which obtains estimates from all the responsible managers. Rather than a "top down" approach, this not only obtains the information from the most knowledgeable sources, but also often connects each manager to his estimates. However, senior management must use their judgment when consolidating a budget prepared by multiple parties. It is not uncommon that the sum of the budgets prepared by managers does not total to an achievable budget relative to the known market conditions or one that reflect senior management's business objectives. (See Exhibit 4-3 to review the typical steps taken in the budgeting process.)

Once you have a budget, you can compare what you're spending with what you expected to spend. If there's a variance, it's a sign that something may be amiss—and you can take appropriate action before it costs you more money. To give a simplistic example, let's say you budgeted $300,000 for payroll, but your actual costs were $350,000. Upon investigation, it turns out that the extra $50,000 came from overtime costs. Now, that might mean poor management, or problems getting materials on time, or downtime on machinery that needs to be looked into. Of course, it might also mean greater-than-anticipated demand.

Any good accounting system will take the budget and actual figures and come up with a report on the variances, as shown in Exhibit 4-4. These budget variances become another kind of early-warning system. As your business grows, the layers of people between you and the product grow as well. Budgeting gives you a way to hold managers who create variances responsible for their performance.

Comparing your budget to actual results also gives you a chance to manage growth. In a sales budget, you estimate what you expect to sell in the future, and you estimate what the cost of selling that much product will be. For instance, let's say you sold 1,000 lamps this year. But you think that next year, you will sell 200 more lamps—1,200 lamps. Those extra 200 lamps don't just represent increased profits; they also represent increased costs. Can you make another 200 lamps without hiring new people? If you do need to add employees, where are they going to work? Will you need more office space or factory space? Perhaps your factory is already working at capacity. Does it pay to open a new factory? How many lamps would you have to sell to justify a new factory? Can you sell that many? The sales budget lets you see what kind of impact the new sales figure is going to have on the whole business.

Any sales budget is dealing with estimates, so caution is advisable. Often, salespeople are optimistic about what they think they are going to sell. So you buy more oil to heat the extra factory space occupied by the workers you've hired to fulfill those 200 additional orders. When those orders fail to materialize, you can end up heating the building for people who aren't there. To guard against overly optimistic or pessimistic budgets, management may consider developing various budget scenarios by varying key budget assumptions. Typically, best case, worst case, and expected case scenarios are devel-

**Exhibit 4-4**

Sample Profit and Loss Report Example Industry: Retail

| | May-97 ACTUAL | % | May-97 BUDGET | % | ACT vs. BUD Variance Amount | % | May-96 ACTUAL | % | This vs. Last Year Variance Amount | % |
|---|---|---|---|---|---|---|---|---|---|---|
| Net Sales | $7,327,531 | 100.00% | $6,657,000 | 100.00% | $670,531 | 10.07% | $5,138,805 | 100.00% | $2,188,726 | 42.59% |
| Cost of Merchandise Sold | (3,296,036) | -44.98% | (2,968,800) | -44.60% | (327,236) | 11.02% | (2,312,947) | -45.01% | (983,089) | 42.50% |
| Gross Profit | 4,031,495 | 55.02% | 3,688,200 | 55.40% | 343,295 | 9.31% | 2,825,858 | 54.99% | 1,205,637 | 42.66% |
| **Direct Stores Expense** | | | | | | | | | | |
| Selling | (1,060,391) | -14.47% | (1,062,800) | -15.97% | 2,409 | -0.23% | (716,580) | -13.94% | (343,811) | 47.98% |
| Occupancy | (584,990) | -7.98% | (609,400) | -9.15% | 24,410 | -4.01% | (478,851) | -9.32% | (106,139) | 22.17% |
| General and Administrative | (313,471) | -4.28% | (364,500) | -5.48% | 51,029 | -14.00% | (193,131) | -3.76% | (120,340) | 62.31% |
| Total Direct Store Expense | (1,958,852) | -26.73% | (2,036,700) | -30.59% | 77,848 | -3.82% | (1,388,562) | -27.02% | (570,290) | 41.07% |
| Operating Income (Loss) | 2,072,643 | 28.29% | 1,651,500 | 24.81% | 421,143 | 25.50% | 1,437,296 | 27.97% | 635,347 | 44.20% |
| **Other Income (Expense)** | | | | | | | | | | |
| Miscellaneous | 1,203 | 0.02% | 0 | 0.00% | 1,203 | 0.00% | 152 | 0.00% | 1,051 | 691.45% |
| Corporate Allocation | (36,858) | -0.50% | (23,500) | -0.35% | (13,358) | 56.84% | (30,497) | -0.59% | (6,361) | 20.86% |
| Home Office Allocation | (682,772) | -9.32% | (754,900) | -11.34% | 72,128 | -9.55% | (531,951) | -10.35% | (150,821) | 28.35% |
| Depreciation and Amortization | (160,040) | -2.18% | (183,800) | -2.76% | 23,760 | -12.93% | (129,838) | -2.53% | (30,202) | 23.26% |
| Total Other Income (Expense) | (878,467) | -11.99% | (962,200) | -14.45% | 83,733 | -8.70% | (692,134) | -13.47% | (186,333) | 26.92% |
| Income (Loss) Before Interest and Taxes | $1,194,176 | 16.30% | $689,300 | 10.35% | $504,876 | 73.24% | $745,162 | 14.50% | $449,014 | 60.26% |

oped. The process of developing budget scenarios is management's first step in planning for contingencies should the Company's actual performance vary from the management's expected scenario.

Top management has to make sure that the budget is realistic. As the budgeting process continues over the years, chronic overestimators will become more apparent, and you can make adjustments based on that experience.

## The Effective Use of a Budget

The jump to developing a budget is an important step in a company's development, but the key second step is using it effectively. The Production Company, a TV and video production business based in three major cities, faced a problem a few years ago that many companies confront: A budget is just a plan, and unexpected events can—and do—occur. Particularly toward the end of the year, a budget formulated more than 12 months before can start looking like ancient history. The market in television and video is extraordinarily competitive, and the fashions that drive sales in this area are notoriously hard to predict. The Production Company's budget, put in place on January 1 for the 12 months through December 31, was sometimes out of date after only six months.

An important function of a budget is to keep expenses in line with anticipated levels of sales. At The Production Company, expenses often exceeded sales widely. This meant that when sales were greater than expected, the budget held back spending money that was really necessary. Larry Marow, the company's president, knew he could no longer watch expenditures at all three locations across the United States.

When he called us, we suggested two concepts. The first is called variable budgeting. In variable budgeting, as sales rise and fall, expenditure levels in certain categories are allowed to rise and fall in proportion to the changing levels of business. By setting up a simple program, Larry's managers would know how much they should spend or should cut back. Managers exceeding these flexible guidelines would have to explain the variance.

The second concept is the roll-forward. Larry knew that budgets developed in November and December more accurately predict the first few months of the year than they do the last few months. This is the case because managers can always predict current sales more accurately than those further off into the future. We recommended a short-term budgeting technique requiring each manager to forecast his next three months. Basically, a roll-forward is a revision of a budget for a foreseeable period—say three months.

Here again, the key principle is comparison. In September, you take your actual results for the year to date, your budget for the year to date, the figures for the current month (from your flash reports), and up-to-date estimates of business going forward. By comparing all these, you can come up with a more accurate estimate of what's going to happen over the short term without relying on an outdated and essentially irrelevant budget. By adding actual results-to-date and a revised budget, you have a much clearer idea of how the year will turn out.

Larry took the suggestion. After two years of this discipline, Larry felt that he knew where his business was going and could avoid the frequent surprises that were so disturbing to him—and to the company's stock price.

The ability to compare and contrast is one of the most powerful tools you have. By comparing your budget to the actual results, you can troubleshoot problems before they become crises. You can also use budgets to compare costs from one year to the next. Two years ago, product development cost you $100,000. This year, after being adjusted for inflation, revenues were the same, but product development costs rose to $125,000. What is that extra $25,000 buying you? Perhaps you have a sensational new product in the offing—or perhaps someone is frittering away your money.

If a company has multiple locations or product lines, these business units can be compared to each other as well. Patterns and trends often become apparent to the practiced eye—and one way an eye becomes practiced is by making these comparisons.

### Benchmarking

Taking it one step further, you can compare your costs and general performance to the costs and general performance of other companies in your industry, a process known as benchmarking. This further step was taken by Larry Marow and The Production Company. Each year Larry had a report prepared using statistics from his trade association.

The report enabled his managers to compare their levels of spending with those of their competitors by expense category, size of competitor, and location.

Many industry associations do financial and operating statistical surveys that track this kind of information. In addition, *The Dun and Bradstreet Industry Norms* and *Business Ratios* publication provides business ratios by SIC code, as does the *Robert Morres Associates, Annual Statement Studies.*

By comparing yourself against other companies in your industry, you can sometimes find out that you're spending more in a specified category than your competition. For example, perhaps you spent 10% on design when everyone else is spending 5%; what are they doing that you're not? This can be a valuable tool in cutting costs and reevaluating assumptions.

You can compare and contrast your performance with that of the most successful companies in your field—the so-called "best in class"—which will allow you to set targets or benchmark. In today's competitive environment, it's not always enough to do a good job. You have to do a better job than the other guy.

Of course, you can't benchmark your performance against that of another company unless you can generate your own information—timely, accurate information that can be broken down and combined in flexible, useful ways. The key to this is an information system. Because in today's business environment, information truly is power.

## ENTREPRENEUR'S SUMMARY

An information system (by which we mean the entire system of people, machines, and methods by which records of business transactions are developed, compared, distributed, analyzed, and acted upon) is one of the most important tools management has. A good information system is both a surrogate for your presence and an early-warning system.

The first principle of an information system is accuracy. Information doesn't do you any good if it's not reliable.

The second principle of an information system is timeliness. In some cases, it's worth sacrificing a little accuracy for a lot of timeliness.

A good information system lets you look at the whole picture by showing you at a glance:

1. *Current performance.* A good information system will generate key financial statistics on profitability, productivity, and liquidity. These include: sales volume and growth; profit margins; working capital and leverage measures; gross profit by customer, product, or service; return on sales; and return on net assets.

2. *How much it costs you to make your product.* Traditional methods of cost accounting have limitations. New methods of cost accounting, such as activity-based costing, can help a company to find its true cost of producing a product and can be crucial in both the pricing and bidding processes.

3. *Inventory.* If you're not allocating costs properly, one of the places it's likely to show up is in inventory. A good information system will allow you to track this vital area, which can mean the difference between success and failure in many expanding businesses.

4. *A budget.* Up until now we've been talking about record-keeping as an enterprise that's historical ("What happened?") and topical ("What's happening right now?"). But a good information system will also enable you to plan for the future. Once you have a budget, you can compare what you're spending with what you *expected* to spend. Looking at the variances allows you to manage growth as well as spot potential problems before they become critical.

5. *Comparisons.* Information systems allow a company to compare its costs and general performance with those of industry leaders. This process, called benchmarking, can be a valuable tool in cutting costs and identifying new opportunities.

# Implementing Information Technology and Controls

We recently took an informal survey of top executives in the service industry, asking them to list their chief priorities for the coming year. Their responses were generally what you might expect: increasing profits, continuing growth, developing and retaining good people. But the fourth highest priority was something of a surprise: to make more effective use of technology.

In the survey, many executives worried most about the seemingly ever-increasing amounts being spent on information technology. They asked, "Are we spending too much?" Others asked another fundamental question: "Are we getting our money's worth?" So we conducted a further survey of these companies to determine their levels of information technology spending, and we found an even more surprising result: None of these companies knew their total information technology costs.

Before you can decide whether or not you're getting your money's worth, it is obvious that you need to know how much you are spending. In one case, we asked the CEO of Comp-U-Tech, the $200-million-a-year computer programming company we described in the last chapter, how much he was spending on information technology. Since he was the head of a high-tech programming company, we weren't surprised that he had the answer right at his fingertips: $1.2 million, a pretty impressive number.

## THE COST OF TECHNOLOGY

Several weeks later, that number had gotten a lot more impressive: The internal audit he'd requested us to make had revealed the figure to be closer to $5 million. Needless to say, the CEO was shocked when we told him. How could they possibly have spent that much? And why didn't he know about it?

In part, it was because we were using a slightly different yardstick. Things are changing so fast in this field that the very definitions of what is part of an information system keeps expanding. What used to be your telephone bill now has to be divided into telephone and telecommunications, both of which come under the rubric of the information system.

Another reason for the discrepancy: Computers and technology have so permeated every facet of the business world that from an accounting standpoint it's difficult to maintain consistent classification of all these expenditures. A while ago, a company might have one big mainframe that was centrally purchased. Today, that company probably has a linked fleet of workstations and PCs on virtually every desk—with many purchases of hardware and services made without central control, or even guidance.

But the biggest reason for the $3.8 million discrepancy between what Comp-U-Tech thought they were spending on information technology and what they were actually spending was that they were looking at direct hardware and software costs and not adding in the indirect costs of any information system: training, outside consultants, internal systems projects, maintenance, etc.

In fact, our survey shows that what most concerns CEOs today is not so much the initial price tag as how much *more* they are being asked to spend every year to maintain their system, update it, and train their staff in its use. And what worries them most is the difficulty of measuring their system's effectiveness.

## THE EFFECTIVENESS OF TECHNOLOGY

How can a company tell if what it's getting from its information technology is worth what it's spending? The traditional yardstick, return on investment, was once the only important measurement of an investment, but today, with the increasing sophistication and pervasiveness of computer technology, there are other measures.

In the era of the mainframe, a CEO might say, "We need to automate our order-processing. How much will that cost?" A team would cost out the price of the mainframe, software and personnel and arrive at a figure. Let's say the figure was $1 million. At that point the CEO might say, "That's a lot of money. What will it do for us?"

"Well," his team might answer, "we will recoup our investment in three years because we'll be able to cut costs and process orders more efficiently. In addition to getting this payback, we'll also be getting more information about our customers: what their buying patterns are, and when they're likely to need additional product."

The CEO would do some computation and decide that the $1 million investment would earn the company a 10% compound rate of return based on a five-year investment period.

But the CEO also knows that the head of sales wants to invest a million dollars in a new product line—and like all salesmen, he's pretty bullish: He's promising a 50% return on the million-dollar investment.

If the CEO only has one million to invest, where should the money go?

## RETURN ON INVESTMENT

A few years ago, the answer was easy: Put it into the project that generates the greatest rate of return.

But these days, the answer is more complicated. First of all, the CEO may have no choice. Customers in certain industries now simply require certain information systems if you want to do business with them. But even if that were not the case, investment in information technology is not always quantifiable. It can contain many hidden benefits that sometimes outweigh the "return on investment" logic that generally guides a company's decisions. These benefits might be assessed, for example, by polling users to see how satisfied they are with the technology, by comparing a company's information technologies with those of industry leaders, and by consulting with experts in the field for advice.

The source of these intangible ROI benefits is the fact that information technology enables a company to improve their efficiency, reduce their costs, and become more productive. It affords companies the opportunity to reexamine their processes and find methods to improve how they do things. Chosen and used properly, information technology isn't just a way to automate a particular function or update existing technology; it's a way for a company to fundamentally redesign its business processes so that they're faster and more efficient and serve the company and its customers better. A company can serve customers better because its employees have the tools to make the right decisions quickly.

Management can analyze the business more effectively with current information. And the company's systems can provide it with a competitive advantage by linking it to its customers and suppliers in what is called the integrated supply chain. In other words, information technology helps a company be better. As information technology has grown more critical, the opportunity cost of *not* investing in it has become so high that a company simply *must* invest in it to stay competitive—even at the expense of short-term profits.

## I.T. METHODOLOGY

Once a company decides it needs to buy new information technology, it may find itself facing what seems at first like a myriad of complicated technical decisions. Should it purchase hardware based on a central CPU or client/server? What operating system should it use? Build the software from scratch or buy ready-made? What kind of database architecture should a new system be based on?

Our advice about these questions may surprise you. It's this: don't think about the technology. That's right—technology is just a tool. What's important about technology is how well it meets your company's needs and how much it allows you to improve your company's processes. We cannot emphasize this enough: The choice of information technology is driven by business needs and process improvement.

Process improvement takes place throughout the four phases of information technology acquisition. These phases are planning, system selection, implementation, and operations. (See Exhibit 5-1.)

**Exhibit 5-1**

Summary Steps—IT Acquisition

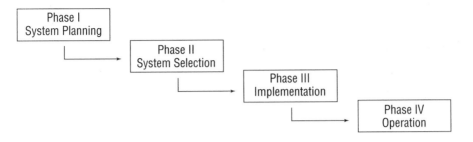

| Phase I | Phase II | Phase III | Phase IV |
|---|---|---|---|
| 1. Assess the current IT situation issues and requirements | 1. For the systems identified in Phase I, develop specific detail requirements | 1. Establish implementation plan | 1. Appoint CIO and develop IT organization, operating procedures and data/ programming controls |
| 2. Determine where the business needs to go - strategic direction and how IT can support this | 2. Develop an RFP or RFI | 2. Develop approach to fill software "gaps" | 2. Develop refresher and advance training plan for new and existing employees |
| 3. Develop an overall IT concept with costs, priorities and technology defined | 3. Distribute and obtain proposals | 3. Revise work process flows | 3. Annually, update the IT plan and budget and monitor throughout the year |
| 4. Develop a detailed IT plan listing projects, costs, timing and resources | 4. Evaluate responses | 4. Implement hardware | 4. Periodically, analyze IT investment by benchmarking vs. competitors, industry standards and customer expectations and evaluating utilization of the existing system's functionality |
| | 5. Select vendors | 5. Initialize software | |
| | 6. Identify major modification requirements | 4. Train users | |
| | 7. Prepare high level implementation plan | 5. Prototype, pilot and test | |
| | 8. Negotiate contract | 6. Introduce revised procedures | |
| | | 7. Cutover | |

In the planning phase, you examine your business (1) to determine what your needs are; and (2) to see if there are ways technology can be used to improve business processes. Each improvement should be related to a business goal. The goal might take the form of streamlining processes to reduce cycle times improving customer service and improving accessibility to information about customers, products, suppliers, and employees. In the next phase, systems selection, you look for a system or a package that will fulfill the needs you've identified. The third step is to implement technology effectively so that you actually get the improvement. Finally, you should operate on a continuous improvement basis to maintain the improvement and take advantage of any additional developments. Obviously, at some point, it will be necessary to consider the technical questions. But these issues should only be considered at the end of the planning stage.

**Phase One: Planning**

Comp-U-Tech came to us because their business was changing. The computer-programming company had been very successful hiring out programmers on a per-man-hour basis—so much so that they started to attract bigger jobs. The bigger jobs had to be bid and executed on the basis of a fixed fee per project. As a result, they desperately needed to acquire an information system that could handle the accounting for project management.

To make the matter more critical, Comp-U-Tech had expanded to 15 other cities in the previous two years. Each office manager had used his own judgment about hardware and software purchases—with the end result that few of the locations' computers could share information. Data had to be manually rekeyed into the general ledger at the home office, which led to delays in basic reporting and a lessened ability to see problems coming. It was clear to management that they had to make a change and make it soon.

When a client comes to us during the planning stage of an information technology purchase, there are two questions we ask: (1) what are the deficiencies in the current system?; and (2) what functions are needed to enable the company to achieve its goals? How does a company go about answering these questions? The first step is to look at the company's overall needs. All too often, a company identifies

---

**Exhibit 5-2**
**Steps in Developing a System Plan**

- Define where the company wants to go—its vision for technology and how it relates to its other business goals (should be part of a Company's Business Plan).
- Define the Company's current I.T. environment—software, hardware, support.
- Assess the issues, bottlenecks and costs of the "as is" state.
- Review the "gaps" between the current situation and the company's goals.
- Develop a blueprint on I.T. strategy, hardware application, software and support, which "best" meets the Company's needs.
- Outline the areas of focus and specify the projects to meet the needs—priorities, timing and approximate costs.
- Develop a plan to carry out the defined strategy listing projects, cost, timing, priority sequence and assign responsible management.

---

one or two pressing needs and stops there. But if a company is about to spend hundreds of thousands or even millions of dollars on technology, it makes sense to look at the technology needs of *all* the company's components and users. Furthermore, as stated earlier, this is often the key to helping the company achieve its strategic plan. (See Exhibit 5-2 to review the major steps in developing a system plan.)

The overall information needs of a business can be determined by internal staff and by outside consultants. It's necessary to speak to all the people in and out of the company who are affected by the information system. That means asking the managers of the different departments how well the current system is handling their needs—and asking them what they wish it *could* do. It means talking to the people in the trenches who use the system every day, and finding out what their frustrations and concerns are. And it may surprise you to learn that it means consulting with the company's clients, customers, and vendors, to find out if they are satisfied with the service provided to them by the company, and how they might improve their ability to work together. The difference between what everyone needs and what they actually have is the gap that the new system would ideally fill. The result of this survey is the basis on which the technology will be chosen. We call it the gap analysis.

For example, we spoke to the marketing and human resource departments at Comp-U-Tech and learned some things that eventually affected the choice Comp-U-Tech made in its new system. Comp-U-Tech often marketed its services to large multidivisional companies. Comp-U-Tech itself had offices scattered around 15 states with little communication between them. So, the company often found itself in a situation where one Comp-U-Tech office was trying to bid a project or sell its services to a division of a company for which another Comp-U-Tech office was already working or for whom they had successfully completed a project. It would obviously be a big help in making the sale if, let's say, the New Jersey office knew that the Chicago office had successfully worked for the prospective client already. This was clearly something a new information system could address—once the need was identified.

The human resources department also had some needs that had not previously been identified. A large part of Comp-U-Tech's business consists of hiring and sending out programmers, so recruitment efforts are crucial. Human resources needed help to recruit sufficient numbers of people with the right skills. Just as the marketing departments of the various Comp-U-Tech branch offices had been unable to coordinate their efforts, the HR offices had also been unable to take advantage of one another's work. If for instance, the New Jersey office had just finished a project that involved 50 C++ programmers, and the Chicago office needed 50 C++ programmers, the Chicago office would have no way of knowing about it.

It may be possible for Comp-U-Tech to solve its other problems at the same time it meets its most immediate needs. Let's suppose that Comp-U-Tech finds itself deciding between two systems. The systems have equally good project management features but one system has a better human resources program than the other. This might make the choice clearer. The needs of the marketing and human resource departments are not Comp-U-Tech's biggest problems right now, but they may be two or three or five years from now. It would be foolish to spend a lot of money solving the problems of today while ignoring the incipient problems of tomorrow.

An essential part of the planning phase is making sure that the technology the company is buying is compatible with its future plans. Does the company intend to start a new business that will require different kinds of software? Are they planning to explore international markets, necessitating currency conversion programs? Do they expect rapid expansion that would require more capacity and sophistication in their data-processing functions?

We often hear new clients complain that the expensive system they bought just a few years ago is already out of date and failing to meet their needs. In addition, the new software they now need often doesn't mesh smoothly with their existing system. The cause of these situations is usually a failure in the planning stages to think through where the company was headed and what its future needs were going to be. It is relatively easy to buy software based on your immediate and pressing needs—but business doesn't stand still; it changes. A company that doesn't anticipate that change can make expensive mistakes.

That's why senior management should always be included in the planning phase. They can give input about the direction in which the company is headed. It's important to make sure that the investment of time and money that an information technology purchase represents is consistent with the direction of the business. If the company has a formal strategic plan, this part of the planning should be straightforward—all that needs to be done is to take a look at the plan and determine how information technology can assist in achieving the new direction. If not, the discussions will have to be longer and more extensive to determine the company's strategy in the first place.

An information technology purchase can't just be about meeting current needs, or even simply about meeting future needs—it must also improve a company's business processes. By buying new technology that is simply faster or that increases capacity, a company's management can miss out on the opportunity to think about how they would have wanted to get that information if they were truly starting from scratch. After all, what's the point of reinforcing problems that already exist?

A good example of this is what almost happened at Picture Perfect, a $20 million company that made picture frames. The accountants at Picture Perfect were overwhelmed trying to keep track of the company's 12 factories. Most of the people in the department were working every night and many were coming in on weekends. Even so, reports were late and budgets weren't getting done. At the CEO's insistence, the company's accountants were trying to figure out how much profit each of the company's 12 factories generated. Since factories are cost centers, not profit centers, this was an approach that not only didn't make sense, but was unwieldy and time-consuming, multiplying much of the work by a factor of twelve. Their current system just couldn't handle this unnecessary transaction volume.

Buying a faster system could have eased but would not have ended Picture Perfect's troubles. The root problem was the way they were doing their accounting in the first place. Rather than buy or build a system that enshrined their inefficient accounting methods, they needed to reexamine and rethink their processes.

This kind of reexamination of business processes should be an integral part of the planning phase. When interviewing the different people in and out of the company to create a gap analysis, it's a good opportunity also to ask some questions: How could this be done better? Is this process necessary? Is there a way to streamline the process? With process improvement, you are looking for a system that will not only solve your immediate need, but help you do things better in the future.

## Phase Two: System Selection

When a company has a clear idea of its needs, it can begin the process of system selection (Exhibit 5-3). As discussed later on, the company may face a make versus buy decision and may need to build a system from scratch but should do so only if appropriate packages do not exist—why reinvent the wheel? System selection starts with a detailed set of specifications of what the company wants and needs in a system. Obviously, the specifications will be guided by the available technology. For instance, a law firm client of ours was looking to improve the effectiveness of their billing system. They didn't realize that data they were entering manually (such as copying costs and phone charges) could be captured automatically using the right software. Once they became aware of this, they immediately changed their specification.

An outside consultant who deals with information systems on a full-time basis can be very helpful in explaining what kind of soft-

**Exhibit 5-3**
Steps in Selecting a System

---

- ❑ For the specific project identified in the System Plan develop detailed functional, technical and operating requirements.
- ❑ Determine selection criteria.
- ❑ Prepare written specifications in an RFP or RFI.
- ❑ Identify viable candidates - either generic or vertical software packages.
- ❑ Distribute RFP/RFI.
- ❑ Analyze vendors responses with high level quantitative and subjective measures: (e.g., open architecture, experience in your industry, technical direction, financial viability, etc.)
- ❑ Develop a "short list" of finalists for detailed evaluation - identify "gaps" in each package and determine approach to fill gap.
- ❑ Attend product demonstrations.
- ❑ Identify system gaps to the Company's specifications and develop requirements for process changes or software modifications.
- ❑ Check references/make site visits.
- ❑ Select package.
- ❑ Layout implementation plan.
- ❑ Negotiate contract.

---

ware is available. Software vendors themselves are excellent information resources, although perhaps not completely objective in judging the merits of rival systems. And information staff within a company are probably not going to be as up-to-date or as familiar with the range of different options as either software vendors or outside systems consultants.

Although the specification will be—or at least should be—based on a knowledge of existing technology, it's not until a company identifies and starts communicating with potential vendors that it will really see what's available on the market. The company's needs and specifications are summarized in an RFP—request for proposal—which is sent out to qualified vendors (see Exhibit 5-4).

In choosing a vendor, the company will, of course, be looking at the vendor's capabilities, price, technical support, and ability to meet the specifications. Other considerations should include the vendor's ability to provide support in implementing the software, the technical direction of the vendor (Is it using R&D to improve the product?) and the stability of the company (Will they be around three

Exhibit 5-4
RFP Table of Contents

# Sample RFP Table of Contents

**Introduction and Company Overview**
**Proposal Instructions**
**Project, Scope, Goals and Objectives**
**Information Technology Environment**
**Transaction Volumes**

**APPENDIX A - Proposal**
    Summary of Proposed Software (Description and Costs)
    Summary of Proposed Hardware (Description and Costs)
    Summary of Proposed Services (Description and Costs)
    Total Cost Summary
    Vendor Qualifications and Background Information
    References
    Product Literature

**APPENDIX B - Response to Functional Requirements**
    General/Technical
    Sales Order Processing
    Inventory Management
    Distribution Management
    Warehousing
    Bill Of Materials
    Forecasting
    Production Planning & Control
    Project Accounting
    General Ledger
    Accounts Receivable
    Accounts Payable
    Fixed Assets

years from now?—a real issue in the software business). It may be that no one vendor can deliver everything the company wants at a price it can afford. In that case, it will probably be necessary to prioritize what's most important. As with any purchasing decision, the chances are that the company will have to compromise.

For example, Comp-U-Tech narrowed its choice down to two

Exhibit 5-4
(Cont/d)

# Topics to Include in an RFP

✓ The Company's project approach & goals
✓ Clearly state the instructions to the vendor for completing the RFP with realistic response times
✓ A brief overview of the Company
✓ Overview of the Company's current IT environment and vision for the future
✓ Provide a list of detailed functional requirements that the Vendor must compare to the capabilities of the proposed version of their software and provide a written response to any functional deficiencies or estimates for proposed modifications
✓ Provide a list of current and expected future transaction and database volumes
✓ Solicit as much information as possible about the vendor, including information on:
    ✓ Financial stability
    ✓ Future development/technology plans
    ✓ Their implementation/modification resources
    ✓ Number of existing customers
    ✓ Pending and past lawsuits
    ✓ Third party relationships
    ✓ Customer references
✓ Obtain specifics on the vendor's proposal for hardware and software, expected implementation assistance, and ongoing maintenance and support
✓ Obtain a cost breakdown for all proposed software, hardware, implementation services and on-going maintenance support

vendors. Both had equally good project-management software, but one had a better human resources package. This vendor was also significantly more expensive. In the end, Comp-U-Tech decided to go with this vendor, but stay within budget by holding off on the purchase and installation of the human resources module of the software package until the next fiscal year. Even without the human resources software, the vendor was still more expensive, but Comp-U-Tech knew it would need the human resources software in the future.

Sometimes a company may find a vendor who can do only part of what it requires and must combine vendors to meet the needs outlined in the RFP.

We found that to be true in the case of The Bradley Group, a financial services firm that handles numerous mortgages and personal loans. They needed a mortgage package, a personal-loan package, and an accounting system. The company went to a variety of vendors and found no one company that had the capability to meet all their needs: one vendor had good mortgage software but didn't have a personal-loan package; in addition, the accounting system wasn't sophisticated enough to handle their operations. Another vendor had a good personal-loan package, but the mortgage and accounting systems weren't acceptable. In the end, The Bradley Group used multiple vendors. They bought the better personal-loan package from one vendor, bought a standard accounting package, and hired the vendor with the superior mortgage software to integrate everything.

Of course, using a single vendor responsible for the entire system is preferable to working with many. Multiple vendors present a complex management problem which, when things go wrong, can degenerate into finger pointing. However, the advantage of working with multiple vendors is that you can get the best of each. To avoid problems, clear definitions of responsibilities need to be established before signing with multiple vendors. In any event, the company should recognize that a decision to use multiple vendors and software products will require more management time and attention in the future.

**Modular Systems.**  While there are some wonderful packages out there that offer simple nuts-and-bolts accounting software, industry leaders have been moving in the direction of modular systems that can be bought in pieces as you need them. Many of these programs begin with an accounting system, but are then backed up with a wide variety of add-ons that enhance the value of the information system without sacrificing compatibility.

For example, many information systems now have add-on modules that are industry-specific: a manufacturing package, a financial-services package, or an insurance package—to name only a few. These software packages are written with specific industries in mind: thus, manufacturing companies can monitor key components such as inventory and integrated product configurations, while financial companies can use such industry-specific tools as multicurrency allocation and graphic representation of financial data. See Exhibits 5-5, 5-6, and 5-7 for modules, key functional requirements, and sample transaction volumes for manufacturing firms.

There are also modules designed not for a specific industry, but for specific tasks, such as project costing and asset management. These modules interact more or less seamlessly with the accounting software. Every module feeds the general ledger, making multiple inputting unnecessary, and making the entire information system that much more timely and accurate.

**Exhibit 5-5.**
Sample List of Software Modules for a Manufacturing and Distribution Company

| |
|---|
| Sales Analysis |
| Order Entry |
| Discounts & Promotions |
| Forecasting |
| Quoting and Estimating |
| Commissions |
| Inventory |
| Warehouse Management |
| Purchasing |
| Manufacturing |
| —Configurator |
| —Bill of Materials (BOM) |
| —Manufacturing Resource Planning (MRP) |
| —Master Production Scheduling (MPS) |
| —Shop floor scheduling |
| —Bar coding |
| General Ledger |
| Accounts Payable |
| Accounts Receivable |
| Foreign Currency |
| Report Writer |
| EDI |

**Exhibit 5-6**
Sample of Key Functional Requirements for a Manufacturing and Distribution
Company

### Sales/Customer Service

- Inventory look-up using matrix
- Automated inventory allocation
- Automated credit screening
- Quotation tracking
- Lead tracking & analysis
- Sales call reporting
- Tracks lost sales
- Tracks configurator sales by materials used and product type
- Marketing database (contact mgt)
- EDI
- Management report writer

### Distribution

- Supports roll goods (width, length etc.)
- Serial # control
- Tracks length remaining on roll
- Tracks product characteristics
- Inventory management
- Facilitates cross-docking
- Facilitates drop shipments
- Able to allocate stock to an order
- Pre-allocate stock to an order
- Bar coding

### Manufacturing

- Integrated MRP & MPS
- Rules based Configurator
- Multi-level BOM
- Finite scheduling
- Work orders generation
- Shop floor control
- Tracks QC inspection results
- Bar coding
- Global change capability
- Management report writer

### Purchasing/Import

- Allocates landed costs to the unit
- Tracks multiple shipment dates
- Tracks shipment & container numbers
- Converts sales orders to multiple purchase orders for drop shipments
- Tracks multiple vendor prices
- Forecasts demand/purchase requirements
- EDI
- Track vendor quality
- Management report writer

### Accounting/Finance

- Integrated A/R, A/P, G/L
- Facilitates team based budgeting
- Multi company/division
- Multi currency
- Specific identification, standard, average, FIFO, LIFO costing
- Automated credit screening
- Collection tickler system
- Bank account reconciliation
- Management report writer

The value of modular software is two-fold. First, it allows a company to grow without making its existing information system obsolete.

As a new information tool becomes necessary, it can be purchased and integrated into the existing system. No one can predict exactly what direction a business is going to grow in, but with a modular system that has a reasonably large library of business modules, you can feel fairly assured that you'll be able to meet even unpredicted needs.

The second value of modular software is that a company does not have to buy an entire system all in one fell swoop. For start-ups, or businesses with cash-flow problems, this can be an important point. However, you may be able to negotiate up front a set price or discount for all the modules.

**Pros and Cons of Using Package Software.** Using the same software as everyone else in your industry means you're no worse

**Exhibit 5-7**

Sample Transaction Volumes

| SALES ORDER PROCESSING | CURRENT | PROJECTED (5 Years) |
|---|---|---|
| Total number of customer accounts | | |
| New customers added to system each month | | |
| Max. number of bill to address records per customer | | |
| Max number of ship to address records per customer | | |
| Average number of quotations entered per month | | |
| Average number of sales orders processed per month | | |
| Average number of line items per order | | |

| BILLING / ACCOUNTS RECEIVABLE (Average number processed each month) | CURRENT | PROJECTED (5 Years) |
|---|---|---|
| Invoices | | |
| Lines per invoice | | |
| Statements | | |
| Cash receipts applied | | |

| ACCOUNTS PAYABLE (Average number processed each month) | CURRENT | PROJECTED (5 Years) |
|---|---|---|
| Invoices | | |
| Voucher / debits / charge-backs | | |
| Payable checks | | |
| Number of banks accounts writing checks from | | |

| PURCHASING | CURRENT | PROJECTED (5 Years) |
|---|---|---|
| Number of vendors in master file | | |
| Purchase orders per month | | |
| Average number of lines per order | | |

| MPS, MRP, BOM | CURRENT | PROJECTED (5 Years) |
|---|---|---|
| Number of finished goods shipped per month | | |
| Maximum number of levels in BOM | | |
| Number of work centers to schedule | | |

| INVENTORY MANAGEMENT | CURRENT | PROJECTED (5 Years) |
|---|---|---|
| Number item masters | | |
| Number of roll goods in stock | | |
| Product classes / types maintained | | |
| Inventory transactions processed per month including picks, put-aways, transfers and returns | | |
| Shipments made per month | | |
| Number of physical warehouses | | |

off, but also no better off, than your competitors. On the positive side, many vendors work hard to offer industry "best practices" so using the software can be an opportunity to make genuine improvements. Also, the best vendors upgrade their software over time incorporating the latest technology. This means system upgrades without major costs or significant disruptions to business. Another advantage is that "standard" software will have many people familiar and trained in its use, thus outside resources will be available to assist with the software as needed. This means continued availability to technical support and continued access to a job market where experienced candidates can be found.

On the negative side, packages are developed to fit many businesses and can often omit capabilities and functions targeted to individual company needs and requirements. And especially with popular software, companies may have to wait a long time to have the vendor deal with specific company problems or requirements.

**Customization.** Certainly, the option exists to design and develop your own system. This can be more expensive and risky than buying and installing a widely-used package, but it gives you capabilities tailored to your individual needs, and provides an advantage over your competition. Management needs to weigh carefully the costs and risks of such a step considering the substantial advantages of the best software companies as noted above. More likely, you may want to go with a solution that is principally package based, with some customization where needed.

Many information system software packages offer some degree of customization, meaning that if your company has a very specific need that is not addressed by the software, then that feature can be added to the system relatively painlessly. This can be something as simple as adding one extra category to an electronic purchase order form or as complicated as linking the information systems of two merging corporations.

Of course, as any freelance computer programmer will be quick to assure you, *any* software can be customized. But while this is *theoretically* true, it makes sense to consider systems that at least support the process—either by providing many customizable features *within* its standard program, or by providing customizing support services itself, or at least by maintaining an open architecture that allows third-party software companies to design customized features for you.

**Will It Work?** Once a company has found a vendor who can give it what it needs, the next step is to make sure the technology will actually work. This involves several critical processes:

*The Feasibility Study.* One way to make sure the system will work is to do a feasibility study. This is especially critical if you're building a system from scratch. That's what Fashion Financial discovered when they went shopping for software. Fashion Financial was a company that did business audits for fashion publications, producing a customized financial statement for each of their clients. They were looking for a system that would enable them to automate the process that prepared financial statements. When they started looking, they had been using a combination of Excel and PageMaker to generate their financial statements. It was a time-consuming process: Data was switched from the client's source to Excel and then from Excel to PageMaker and then the operator spent more time fitting everything in. Fashion Financial thought that surely there was a better way.

However, it turned out that there was no package in the marketplace that did what they needed. They decided to create their own system and found a vendor to design it for them. They were all ready to spend half a million dollars when we suggested doing a feasibility study. Sure enough, the feasibility study indicated that they were not going to get what they wanted. The problem was that they simply had too many mutually exclusive requirements. Basically, Fashion Financial was customizing a financial statement for each individual client. No two clients submitted the same data, nor did they submit it in the same form, nor were the financial statements of any two clients formatted in exactly the same way. It would take a gigantic amount of programming to handle the job, if it even could be done. To us, this indicated a high development cost.

However, the mandate from Fashion Financial was that the price had to be kept down, or the new system had to yield dramatic savings to offset the price. As a membership organization, Fashion Financial couldn't pass on any significant increase to its members or ask them to incur additional costs that might make the process more uniform.

The importance of a feasibility study is underlined by the fact that everyone in the situation we've just described was acting professionally and in good faith. The vendor's salespeople and engineers honestly believed they could do the job—they're part of a programming company, operating from the premise that there's nothing technology can't do. And Fashion Financial had thought through its specification in an effort to find a better way to do business.

Yet without a feasibility study, Fashion Financial was heading toward the money pit, throwing good cash after bad in an attempt to engineer the impossible. This type of experience usually ends with everyone sitting around the table looking at each other and asking, "How did we get into this mess in the first place?"

*Vendor Package Support.* The best information system software in the world would quickly become useless without continued support, so it pays to choose a system that is continually updated, maintained, and serviced. Most of the systems software companies understand how important this is, and vie to provide what one company describes as "positively outrageous customer support."

We saw an example of the importance of customer support when one of our clients, an insurance brokerage, purchased a system software package oriented for insurance brokers. It was a great program, designed to work both with traditional midrange computers as well as with a variety of high-end Unix hardware systems. Our client was very happy with the software—until the software supplier got into financial difficulties and decided it could no longer support the state-of-the-art hardware our client had bought at great expense.

Since most of the software company's clients had the older midrange systems, this was a good call for the software company, but it left our clients out in the cold. The obvious lesson is that it's important to choose software whose vendor has a reputation for standing behind its product, who is in strong financial shape, and who already has a substantial number of referenceable users. You can screen out the less desirable packages by calling potential vendors and obtaining basic information needed to make a choice. (Exhibit 5-8 is a sample questionnaire that can be used as a guide during a vendor call.)

*The Demo.* Another way to ensure that your system will work is to stay focused on your requirements during a demonstration of the software. Remember, for the vendor, the demo is a sales tool. He'll pull out every bell and whistle he has to make the sale. Whatever the vendor shows you, your response should always be, "How does this meet my requirements?" Use your list of requirements from the RFP as a checklist to validate vendor suitability. This may seem obvious, but if you remember shopping for your first stereo system, and giving serious consideration to the purchase of six-foot-tall speakers with "world class" sound for your studio apartment, then you'll also re-

## Exhibit 5-8
Sample Vendor Screening Questionnaire (Example Industry: Manufacturing/
Distribution)

Company: _____   Package: _____
Contact: _____   Phone: _____
Title: _____   Date: _____

### VENDOR INFORMATION

1) What type of software products do you sell?
2) What were your 1996 sales dollars? How much of those sales dollars were for software?
3) How many total employees do you have? How many R&D personnel? How many Technical/implementation consultants?

### TECHNICAL ENVIRONMENT

1) What database(s) does your software support?
2) Which hardware platforms does your software run on?
3) What type of client workstations are needed to run the software (PCs or dumb terminals)?
4) What languages and development tools has the code been developed in?
5) Can the source code be purchased and modified by customers?
6) What type of development training is available for customers?
7) Describe the technical documentation available to customers?

### SOFTWARE FEATURES

1) What modules are integrated with your software and modules have you interfaced with third party packages before?

|  |  | Name of 3rd Party Pkg. |
|---|---|---|
| ❑ | Order processing | _____ |
| ❑ | Sales analysis | _____ |
| ❑ | Inventory management | _____ |
| ❑ | Forecasting | _____ |
| ❑ | EDI | _____ |
| ❑ | G/L | _____ |
| ❑ | A/P | _____ |
| ❑ | A/R & billing | _____ |
| ❑ | Report writer | _____ |
| ❑ | Query tools | _____ |
| ❑ | Other: _____ | _____ |
| ❑ | Other: _____ | _____ |

2) Does your software facilitate inventory lookup, during order entry, based on item characteristics (e.g., size, shape)?
3) Does your software support lot and serial control of inventory items?
4) How many warehouses does your software support?
5) Does your software support consignment inventory for multiple warehouses?
6) How many companies and divisions does your software support?
7) Is your software fully integrated to the accounting modules (or interface with third party accounting packages)?

### VENDOR SUPPORT

1) Do you provide implementation assistance? If yes, explain.
2) Who supports the software after implementation? (Do you have a hot-line service?)
3) Are there periodic user group meetings. If yes, explain.
4) How often are you releasing new versions of the software? When are the next schedule version releases and what features or functionality will be added or improved?
5) Is the software documentation updated to reflect new versions/releases of the software?

member how easy it is to get caught up in technical wonders even though they're not relevant to your needs.

*Reference Checks.*   When a company has narrowed its choices down to two or three vendors, it's a good idea to do a reference check. Reference checks are one of the key steps in the system-selection phase. In a reference check, the vendor introduces the buyer to a current owner who is using the same system. In most cases, the vendor will accompany the prospective customer to the current customer's workplace to see the system in action. These "tours" are an excellent way of checking out the vendor's software. We've accompanied many clients on such tours and there's usually a lot of spirited and informative shoptalk exchanged. In several cases, clients had been undecided between different options, and found discussing the choice with someone in the same business who was actually using the software to be critical in reaching a decision. (Exhibit 5-9 is a sample reference questionaire for a company in the manufacturing or distribution industry.)

*Prototyping.*   Further down the road, developing a prototype provides another opportunity to make sure you're going to get what you need. A prototype allows you to see exactly what computer screens are going to look like. We had one client, Amity Insurance, who took advantage of this step. They needed a way to track certain kinds of accounts that they wanted to group together and sell off to another insurance company. We had mock-ups of the database and report screens made using a program called Screen Painter. The screens weren't hooked up to the company's system, so there was no information being entered or processed, but the client was able to sit down at the screen to see how it looked. Looking at the prototype, Amity realized that some of the data they wanted in the reports was information they had not asked for in the specification. Ultimately, the database plan was reconfigured and the new system screens were designed based on the refined mock-up.

After prototyping, but before you sign with a vendor, you can do a conference room pilot. The vendor will take some of your data and load it onto the system and run it through. This too can be an opportunity to make adjustments and changes to bring the system into closer sync with your requirements.

## Exhibit 5-9

Sample Vendor Reference Questionnaire (Example Industry: Manufacturing/ Distribution)

Company: _____  Package: _____
Contact: _____  Phone: _____
Title: _____  Date: _____

### COMPANY INFORMATION

1) What type of products do you sell?

2) How many employees do you have?  How many users do you have?

3) How many different companies and/or division do you have?

4) How many manufacturing plants and/or warehouse locations do you have?  Do you use public warehouses?

5) Do you have distribution operations?

6) Do you have operations or sales outside of the U.S.?

7) What are your Company's annual sales revenue?

8) What software did you use prior to this software package?

9) Describe your MIS Department (e.g., # of employees and skill sets).

### SOFTWARE IMPLEMENTATION

1) When did you purchase the software?

2) What modules have you implemented and which ones were third party packages?

|  |  | Name of 3rd Party Pkg. |
|---|---|---|
| ❑ | Warehouse/inventory management | _____ |
| ❑ | Distribution resource planning (DRP) | _____ |
| ❑ | Bar coding | _____ |
| ❑ | Material requirements planning (MRP) | _____ |
| ❑ | Order processing | _____ |
| ❑ | Sales analysis | _____ |
| ❑ | Purchasing | _____ |
| ❑ | Importing | _____ |
| ❑ | Forecasting | _____ |
| ❑ | Telemarketing | _____ |
| ❑ | EDI | _____ |
| ❑ | Cost accounting | _____ |
| ❑ | G/L | _____ |
| ❑ | A/P | _____ |
| ❑ | A/R | _____ |
| ❑ | Report writer | _____ |
| ❑ | Query tools | _____ |
| ❑ | Other: _____ | _____ |

3) How long did it take to implement the software?  When was your implementation completed (i.e., when did you "go live")?

4) Did the implementation follow the original schedule and cost estimates?

5) What was the makeup and skill level of the implementation team?

6) How were the implementation tasks phased?

7) What implementation tasks were provided by the vendor and which implementation tasks did you do in-house?

8) Did the same software vendor employees stay with the project from start to finish?  What was the level of vendor management oversight?  Were there any key vendor project staff or managers you would recommend?

9) Did the vendor provide guidance and insights in terms making enhancements to your operations in order to make the best use of the system?

10) What software errors have you encountered?  If any, did the vendor correct the problems adequately?

11) Do you have access to the source code?  If so, have you made changes to the code?

**Exhibit 5-9**
(Cont'd)

12) Custom modifications:
   - What modifications or enhancements were done to the software?
   - Who wrote and tested the modifications?
   - Do the modifications perform as anticipated?
   - Were they implemented on time and within the initial cost estimates?
   - Were they tested and documented?

13) What user documentation was provided by the vendor? How useful is it? Was additional documentation required? If so, who wrote it?

14) How useful is the on-line help?

15) What type of training was provided to the users? How many days were devoted to each module?

16) How effective was the training? Was additional training required?

17) What were some unforeseen problems encountered during the implementation?

**HARDWARE IMPLEMENTATION**

1) What hardware platform are you using? What was your basis for choosing this hardware?

2) Who installed the hardware? How would you rate their performance?

3) Have you had to upgrade the hardware? If so, why?

4) Is the performance of the hardware adequate?

5) What hardware problems did you encounter?

**ONGOING VENDOR SUPPORT**

1) What has been the vendor's attitude towards service after the sale?

2) Who is supporting the software now?

3) How do you typically notify the vendor of system problems and what methods does the vendor use to respond to them?

4) What is the typical time to fix a problem?

5) How have software upgrades (e.g., new versions) affected you? Have the upgrades offered significant improvements in features and/or performance?

6) Has the documentation been updated to reflect modifications and new versions of the software?

7) How responsive has the vendor been to additional modifications/enhancements that you have requested after the implementation was complete?

**OVERALL SATISFACTION**

1) How would you rate the software on a scale of 1 (worst) to 10 (best)?

2) What have been the software package's strongest and weakest points? What have been your biggest frustrations with the software?

3) How would you rate the vendor implementation services and ongoing support services on a scale of 1 (worst) and 10 (best)?

4) What are the vendor's strongest and weakest points?

5) If you could do it again, would you select the same software package?

6) What implementation steps would you do differently?

**The Contract.** The final step of the decision-making process is putting it all down on paper: the contract. Unfortunately, many standard information system software contracts start out one sided. Often, they have been drawn up and presented by the *vendor* and address the vendor's concerns for protection of rights. Naturally, this first draft of the contract is only a place from which to begin. Like all contracts, a system software contract should spell out, in writing, all the rights and responsibilities of both parties. And any company buying an information system must keep their entire relationship with the vendor in mind—from licensing to acquisition to maintenance—while looking as far into the future as possible. (See Exhibit 5-10 for possible contract terms to consider.)

Whole books can be written about contracts, and the issue gets technical and specific very quickly. However, there are two things of which any company that is buying information technology should be aware. The first is to pay close attention to when payments are required. There are different ways of structuring a contract, but at least some of the payment should be held back and tied to performance.

The second is to append to the contract a copy of the vendor's response to the RFP—which, you'll remember, is your specification and the vendor's proposal. The contract should state that the vendor has to meet the terms of the proposal. This legally obligates the vendor to meet the specification agreed to in the proposal.

In any event, it always makes sense to seek the advice of counsel before signing a significant systems contract. As information technology has become widespread, disputes between users and vendors have become frequent. Certain law firms specialize in systems contracts and should be retained to protect the user and limit his risks, especially in the development of custom software.

## Phase Three: Implementation

When the newly purchased system arrives, the implementation process begins. Implementation involves installing the new system, converting the old system to the new system, testing it, and training staff to run it.

However, before implementation takes place, it's crucial that an implementation plan be drawn up. (Exhibit 5-11 highlights the major tasks that may be included in an implementation plan.)

The plan should list every step necessary for the system to become operational, who is responsible for each step, and when each step will take place. In this way everyone knows what their responsibility is and by when they need to get things completed.

Just because a company has an implementation plan does not guarantee that everything will run smoothly or take place on

**Exhibit 5-10**

Possible Contract Terms for Software Purchases

◇ Payment schedule which provides for periodic payments after completion of certain milestones, such as successful conference room pilot and successful acceptance testing after full implementation. (Example payment schedule: 25-33% down, 33-50% after installation and demonstration, remainder paid after acceptance testing)

◇ Provision for acceptance testing, after which the final payment will be made. For example, allow for a 60 day time period to use and test all critical features of the software.

◇ Implementation timetable, which includes specific dates and activities

◇ Maintenance and warranty coverage period, with consideration for third party software

◇ Specify training to be provided and the associated costs in terms of what, where, how, and when

◇ Pricing of modules not currently purchasing (but may be required in the future), as well as the cost of upgrading to later versions when they become available

◇ Vendor performance measures, such as response time window

◇ Definition regarding successful software implementation

◇ Identify who will integrate new hardware and software with existing systems.

◇ The maximum number of concurrent users, including the definition of a concurrent user

◇ Software configuration and version

◇ Assurance that the software package will run under the existing or expected hardware and network configuration (include attachment of hardware listing and note server)

◇ Source code availability pending bankruptcy or loss of VAR (Value Added Reseller) status

◇ Confidentiality clause covering the Company's data and shared documents

◇ Permission to copy the software onto a backup machine if necessary for Disaster Recovery

◇ Vendor's rights to sell the software, including indemnification where rights do not exist

◇ Rights to relocate the software to new facilities or entities

◇ Single source contract for all software, hardware, maintenance and implementation services

**Exhibit 5-11**

Sample Tasks Associated with Implementing a Computer Based Information System

**Project Management**

- Provide oversight and guidance to management
- Moderate key project planning and status meetings
- Intervene with vendors as needed
- Monitor project activities & milestones
- Prepare periodic status reports
- Maintain Issues Log
- Develop training schedule
- Maintain project performance measures
- Maintain budget analysis

**Project Planning**
- Determine project organization
- Develop measurable project goals
- Develop detail project plan and budgets
- Assign resources
- Develop detailed Network Plan

**Hardware & Software Installation**
- Install hdwr, network & software
- Performance tune and test
- Develop & document IS operating procedures

**Business Process Definition & System Pilot**
- Develop pilot/process modeling plan
- Facilitate team-based pilot workshops
- Develop operational objectives & performance measures
- Review functional flow of the system and develop process definitions
- Document policies & procedures for each process
- Test sample transactions
- Identify software gaps and evaluate alternatives

**Implementation Team Training**
- Classroom training
- Individual exercises
- ID operational /system issues

**Data Conversion**
- Develop data map/ conversion reqmnts
- Design, develop and test conversion programs (if req'd)
- Test & modify
- Convert & load data

**Software Enhancements & Integration**
- Identify 3rd pty pkgs & mods (e.g., EDI, bar-code)
- Develop specs, purchase, program, install & test

**End User Training**
- Classroom training
- Individual exercises
- Train users on new procedures

**Organization Readiness Assessment**
- Design user readiness tests customized for the Company's operations
- Test users on new software and procedures
- Test MIS operating procedures
- Evaluate organization's confidence in new systems

**Software Readiness Assessment**
- Design software tests
- Test software vs. Company's procedures and data

**Go-Live**
- Evaluate accuracy of data
- Evaluate operating procedures
- Develop action plan and prioritize
- Implement and document required changes
- Evaluate use of system
- Develop plan to optimize investment going forward

time—but it does mean that if there are delays or problems, whatever actions are necessary to correct problems and speed things up will be swiftly taken.

Without an implementation plan, the company runs the risk of having the changeover to new system software drag on. Months can pass in this way, and an atmosphere of "it's not my job, it's his job," can begin to prevail. Meanwhile, the company isn't receiving the benefits of increased productivity and efficiency for which the system was purchased.

The implementation phase provides opportunities to improve business processes. There may be some process improvements that have been planned that cannot actually be executed until the system is up and running. For instance, if a new program for automated customer credit checks has been purchased, it will not be possible to reorganize and streamline the credit check department until the new system has been implemented.

Of course, the best information system in the world will be useless if it isn't working properly. To confirm that the new system is functioning accurately, we always recommend that a series of checks be made. Although it would be ideal if the old and new systems could be run parallel, this is not always possible. However, once the new system is in place, data from the previous month can be run through it to make sure that the new system generates the same or better information as the old system.

As much as you don't want the process to drag on, moving too fast can also result in trouble. If you try to convert too quickly and skimp on training, your employees may feel uncomfortable with the new system, data may be entered incorrectly by the rank and file, and information may be interpreted incorrectly by managers, leading to bad decisions.

During the conversion process, the tendency is to rely on the technical support of the software makers or that of outside consultants. Valuable as they are, it should be remembered that these people are eventually going to go home, leaving your workforce on its own. So it's very important that your staff learn and absorb the information provided by the outside technical support you've brought in.

## Phase Four: Day-to-Day Operations

The personnel responsible for the day-to-day operations of a modern information system have been thrust into a limelight no one could possibly have imagined a few years ago. In the old days, computer personnel were shut away with the mainframe in the computer room. Today—when the first experience the public at large has of a company may well be its web page—the judgment, competence, and integrity of information system personnel have become that much more critical.

All this speaks for the need of a senior executive in the organization with a business-wide viewpoint: a chief information officer responsible for all aspects of information technology. Spreading this responsibility around among several people, even if they are responsible for different divisions or strategic business units, tends to dilute the force of the decision making. It also risks a noncohesive policy in which different units use noncompatible software. The CIO will ensure that information technology becomes an item on every annual review agenda. He will also make sure that when the system gets an upgrade or a new feature, it will be announced and explained to the relevant personnel in the company. Upgrades and new software features can't benefit a company if employees aren't aware of their existence and trained in their use.

As operational issues arise, the CIO will be responsible for overseeing their solution. Once the system is up and running there will be many competing demands on the information technology department. For instance, the head of sales may say that he's selling more product over the Internet than anticipated, and he needs a way to keep track of those sales. That would mean a new program would have to be acquired, installed and tested, and employees trained in its use. And there may be many requests like this from various departments of the company. The information technology department will probably not have enough people, time, or money to do everything asked of it immediately.

How does the CIO keep abreast of everyone's needs? How does he know which ones should receive priority? We think the best approach is to have a steering committee that represents all the major areas of the company and meets regularly to discuss issues cross-functionally and set priorities. Such a committee is often chaired by the president or chief operating officer, who must make sure that everyone's priorities are met. The priorities, of course, have to be linked back to the cost of technology and its effectiveness. The CIO will have to balance meeting the company's needs with what the company can afford, while staying focused on continuous improvement. The decisions he makes will have a broad effect on the company and, ideally, he should be reporting as high up as possible in the organization. We've seen some steering committees chaired by the CEO himself—which gives you some idea of the importance many companies assign to information systems.

Unfortunately, as the importance of the information system has grown, the skills of the persons originally assigned to head up these systems may not have kept pace.

At Amity Insurance, Sam Lear was in charge of information technology. Sam was a computer wiz from the very early days of information systems. He was very much at home with technology, but less comfortable with the people who had to use the systems he maintained. Amity's information system was a mix-and-match amalgam of different software products that had been adequate in the 1980s but was beginning to show its age. It was time to modernize, but Sam was resisting. We went to trade shows with him to look at possible software programs. The new programs were mainly Windows-based, but Sam was attracted to one of the few menu-based programs, and said, "now *this* is a program."

When he was outvoted, and a new Windows-based piece of software was purchased, Sam brought in a young assistant to manage the new software while he supervised the old software. In other words, Sam had stopped performing his primary responsibility as an information officer. The first priority of any information manager is to operate a system that best serves the company. Ease of use has to be one of the more important features to consider in a program designed to be operated by a constantly changing roster of personnel.

Even when a chief information officer is a technological genius, a lack of people skills can eventually negate all of his talent. The CIO at Cross Apparel is a good example. Bill Upton was brilliant, but myopic. He made sure everything ran like clockwork, but never took time to talk to the people who used his system. For example, as part of his duties, he helped to design a web site for the company's traveling sales reps. The site was a thing of beauty and a technological marvel, but the sales people found it awkward and counterintuitive to use. Needless to say, Bill had not consulted with the people who would actually use the web site before he designed it. Bill was simply not accessible, and after a while, people gave up trying to communicate with him. A CIO who is caught up in the minutiae of information technology to the exclusion of the dissemination of information is of no real value—and Cross Apparel eventually decided to hire someone who was willing to look at the big picture.

## DISASTER RECOVERY

At some point in every company's life, the big picture will involve either the threat of or actual catastrophic loss of an information system. When people hear the words "disaster recovery" they automatically think of computer crashes or viruses—but disaster recovery is not just a computer issue. An information system is much more than hardware and software. The bombing of the World Trade Center brought this home in a real way to many companies.

If an earthquake takes out your San Francisco office on Tuesday, do you have a plan in place that will have that office up and running on Wednesday in another location? Or, in a slightly more likely circumstance, do you have a plan if there's a power outage or electrical fire at one of your sites?

Answering this question in the affirmative means that you have thought about a much wider range of issues than just computers. Office space, replacement workers, phone lines, insurance—these are only some of the elements that go into a fully developed contingency plan.

On the computer front, the simplest and most central concept is to back up data at the end of each day, and to store backups off site. We know of one small single-site company that rigorously backed up all its computers each day by transferring the contents of one hard drive onto the other, and so on. After all, they reasoned, what were the odds that more than one hard drive would fail at a time? The office was completely destroyed in a fire one morning. All company records that had not been duplicated by the company's accounting firm were lost forever.

To avoid this kind of scenario, companies have to plan ahead.

We have one client located in a Florida flood zone. When management decided to build a second location, they initially chose a site located in another flood zone. We talked them out of that. A secondary site is not just a chance to expand market share and revenues; it's a chance to store your vital information in a completely different environment, thereby reducing the odds that a natural disaster will destroy both sets of data.

But the real test of a disaster-recovery plan is how often it is tested. Most companies *have* a plan, but if you were to ask one of your employees at random what his duties would be in the event of a disaster, would he know? Each year, all disaster scenarios should be run through with all personnel. These run-throughs are not much different than a basic fire drill. The scenarios should run the gamut from a server crash to a minor flood to a major act of war.

Of course, not all disasters are natural. Nowadays, your data is as likely to be threatened by a computer virus as a fire or weather disaster.

We're often asked if computer viruses are really something a company should worry about. Do your employees bring in their own diskettes to work and run them on your system? Is information from the Internet being downloaded onto your system? Of course, the answers to these questions are yes, and so is the answer to whether you should worry about viruses. It only takes one "infected" piece of information from outside your system to corrupt your data. Therefore, employees should be prohibited from bringing their own diskettes into work. In any event, virus-protection software that searches out and destroys the virus should be purchased and used. (Exhibit 5-12 provides a detailed approach to performing a disaster recovery planning project.)

## SECURITY

As Internet and Intranet applications grow, the potential for loss of information to hackers or even industrial espionage grows as well. Most information system software comes with passwords and rudimentary input and output controls—and these may well suffice to protect your information as long as you have no telecommunications. But as soon as you begin talking about multiple sites with computers

**Exhibit 5-12**

Disaster Recovery Planning Project (Sample Approach)

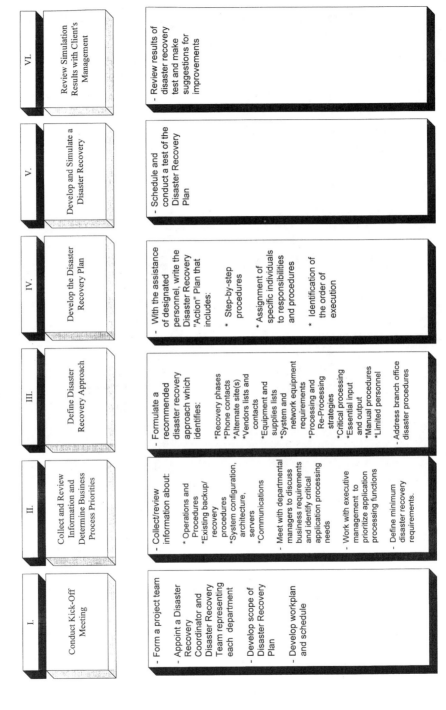

| I. Conduct Kick-Off Meeting | II. Collect and Review Information and Determine Business Process Priorities | III. Define Disaster Recovery Approach | IV. Develop the Disaster Recovery Plan | V. Develop and Simulate a Disaster Recovery | VI. Review Simulation Results with Client's Management |
|---|---|---|---|---|---|
| - Form a project team<br><br>- Appoint a Disaster Recovery Coordinator and Disaster Recovery Team representing each department<br><br>- Develop scope of Disaster Recovery Plan<br><br>- Develop workplan and schedule | - Collect/review information about:<br>  * Operations and Procedures<br>  * Existing backup/recovery procedures<br>  * System configuration, architecture, servers<br>  * Communications<br><br>- Meet with departmental managers to discuss business requirements and identify critical application processing needs<br><br>- Work with executive management to prioritize application processing functions<br><br>- Define minimum disaster recovery requirements. | - Formulate a recommended disaster recovery approach which identifies:<br>  * Recovery phases<br>  * Phone contacts<br>  * Alternate site(s)<br>  * Vendors lists and contacts<br>  * Equipment and supplies lists<br>  * System and network equipment requirements<br>  * Processing and Re-Processing strategies<br>  * Critical processing<br>  * Essential input and output<br>  * Manual procedures<br>  * Limited personnel<br><br>- Address branch office disaster procedures | - With the assistance of designated personnel, write the Disaster Recovery "Action" Plan that includes:<br><br>  * Step-by-step procedures<br><br>  * Assignment of specific individuals to responsibilities and procedures<br><br>  * Identification of the order of execution | - Schedule and conduct a test of the Disaster Recovery Plan | - Review results of disaster recovery test and make suggestions for improvements |

115

that can talk to each other, even if you are communicating via the Internet, then you have to start thinking in terms of more advanced protection.

The topic of information system security is really a book unto itself; there is no room here to do justice to this vital topic. Suffice it to say that firewalls (code-based walls designed to keep Internet visitors out of the secure parts of the information system) are vital. And these firewalls must be constantly maintained and monitored by experts.

## THE COST OF PROGRESS

The price tag on all this maintenance, software updates, new hardware, and continual training can be high, but here are some ways to contain the costs:

*Spend in Annual Increments.* Make information technology expenditures in annual increments rather than in one fell swoop. This allows the business to "average" the latest technology with prior years' technology.

In a way, picking information technology really is like picking stocks—it is nearly impossible to be a winner every time. However, by making annual expenditures, you prevent any mistake from taking on huge dimensions. We've seen companies buy all Macintosh computer hardware only to realize a year or two later that they really needed to be compatible with their IBM-supplied customers. We've seen companies make huge hardware purchases only to find that the software they really need is incompatible with the hardware. And we've seen companies throw away perfectly fine system software and hardware too, in an effort to be totally up to date, even when it was not necessary. By purchasing annually, the odds of making any of these mistakes decrease. For example, if your company owns a fleet of aging 486 computers, replace only a third of them with newer models this year. Then, next year (when, inevitably, some faster and even better chip will have been invented), you can replace another third—and so on.

Making purchases in stages instead of all at once can prevent your company from making costly errors in judgment, allow employees to get used to new software gradually rather than having to learn an entire system all at once, and give management the time to take a good long look at the different system-software packages available.

*Don't Buy the Latest and Greatest.*   When making a major information technology purchase, the temptation is to get the latest model. After all, as the salesperson will point out, the pace of change is rapid. Why not protect your investment by getting the very latest thing?

There are actually several compelling reasons. For one, sometimes the new product that is just out of the factory door does not work very well. This is particularly true of software that may have bugs you would much prefer someone *else* to discover and deal with.

For another, the very latest thing usually costs a lot more money, at least initially. When a software or hardware company is trying to amortize its initial development expenses, the price of the latest cutting-edge software is going to stay high. Fortunately, as computer capacity rises, prices fall almost as fast, on both hardware and software. Thus, if you buy just behind the curve, you can get 90% of the advantage at 50% of the cost.

*Don't Build It from Scratch.*   There is a reason why we make fun of people who try to reinvent the wheel: It took a lot of energy and money to invent in the first place. In most cases, a company is better off buying a package than designing an information system from scratch. After all, why not take advantage of all that thought and energy and R&D paid for by other companies?

Certainly, the thought of a system that has been created solely for your own company can seem very alluring. If the system were truly innovative, you might obtain a real advantage over your competitors either by getting faster reads on the overall marketplace or by getting faster internal reports from within the company. An innovative design might increase efficiency and create faster response times to the customer's needs.

On the other hand, if the system doesn't perform as well as expected, your company would be way behind—and you wouldn't really know this until after it was designed, installed, and paid for. With a well-known, well-supported software package, you know what you're getting in advance. And with all the industry-specific modules being designed today, and the customizing features that are a standard part of many software packages, you can have an information system that feels very much tailored to your individual situation.

*Don't Forget the Human Factor.* It's an all-too-common mistake. A company sets up a team to research information software. The team does an excellent job of pinpointing the company's information needs; the right software is found; a good price is negotiated; a half million dollars is spent.

And then they plunk the new system down on people's desks and walk away, somehow expecting them to be able to use it.

The single information system cost that consistently gets ignored is people-related: the money for training, the money to bring in outsiders and specialists when needed, the money for service and support.

It's not unusual for one third of an information system budget to be spent on the human side. Probably the most important part of that money will be spent not on outsiders or support calls, but on the people within the company who must work with the system every day. If these employees are fully trained in the features of the software, they will be able to exploit it to its fullest.

If not, they could end up like a direct-mail company we know who almost replaced a system that they didn't need to replace. The company thought their old system, which they had installed ten years earlier, was outmoded. After all, every time they went to Sheila, a former secretary to whom they had given the responsibility of running the system, and asked for a statistic or item of information, she would say that the system didn't generate it.

The company was on the brink of buying new system software when a customer-support person from their about-to-be-former software company realized what was going on: Sheila had not kept abreast of nearly 10 years worth of enhancements and add-ons. When each new version of the software arrived, Sheila would install it, but she never explored its new features, and didn't attend any of the training seminars where she might have learned to use them.

In fact, the software was still more than adequate for the direct-mail company's needs. The lesson here is not just that the software has to stay current, but that the people who run it and use it have to stay current with the software. Without adequately trained people to run it, the best information technology will be useless.

## THE BIG PICTURE

Information technology is just a tool to help you run your business. Like any tool, it has to be used correctly. And like any tool, it must be chosen with care so that you have the right tool for the job. What makes an information technology system right for your business is the extent to which it meets your business' needs. No matter how sophisticated or advanced the system, if it doesn't meet your company's needs it's not the right system for you.

In today's world, it is inevitable that every company faces major expenditures for information technology. If you keep in mind that the technology has to meet the needs of your company, you will greatly increase the chances of a successful purchase—a purchase that makes your company more productive, efficient, and, ultimately, more profitable.

## ENTREPRENEUR'S SUMMARY

### I. The Cost and Effectiveness of Technology

Entrepreneurs today are concerned by the ever-increasing cost of technology, and worried about the effectiveness of technology in which they have invested. Unfortunately, in trying to measure that effectiveness, the classic yardstick—return on investment—is no longer the sole criteria for making information technology decisions.

Information technology enables companies to improve their efficiency, reduce costs, and become more productive. It affords companies the opportunity to reexamine their processes and find methods to improve how they do things. As information technology has grown more critical, the opportunity cost of *not* investing in it has become so high that a company simply *must* invest in it to stay competitive—even at the expense of short-term profits.

### II. The Process of Technology Acquisition

Once a company decides it needs to buy new information technology, it may find itself facing what seems at first like a myriad of complicated technical decisions, but it is a mistake to think about the technology itself. Rather, a company should focus on what it wants the technology to do, and use this as an opportunity to rethink its critical processes.

Process improvement takes place throughout the four phases of information technology acquisition:

1. In the planning phase, you examine your business (i) to determine what your needs are, and (ii) to see if there are ways technology can be used to improve business processes.

2. In the system-selection phase, you look for a system or a package that will fulfill the needs you've identified. The process begins with the design of a detailed specification, a feasibility study, reference checks, a demonstration, and prototyping of essential computer screens.

3. During the implementation phase, the new system is installed and tested, and employees are trained.

4. In the operations phase, a company should operate on a continuous-improvement basis to train employees in the use of the information technology, to maintain the system, and to take advantage of any additional developments in technology. The appointment of a CIO is a crucial part of this process.

## III. Disaster Recovery and Security Issues

When people hear the words "disaster recovery" they automatically think of computer crashes or viruses—but disaster recovery is not just a computer issue. An expanding company should have contingency plans for the loss of physical plants and key personnel, as well as computer systems. It should also have security for its information.

# Planning for Succession

The day Sarah James took over her father's business was the worst day of her life.

It was January 2nd—four days after her father's death. Paul James had been in ill health for years, but he still ran James Electronics with an iron fist. Sarah found it hard to believe he was gone. As the child with the most business experience, she had been the logical choice among her siblings to assume the presidency. She walked into her father's office, sat down in his chair behind his desk, and started going through the books.

James Electronics was primarily a Defense Department contractor. Sarah had been vaguely aware that business had been off for the past several years, but her father had never been one to discuss company matters with the family. Now Sarah was faced with the truth: Sales were down 50% over the previous six years. The company had lost money during each of the previous five years. Her father had been keeping the business afloat with funds he withdrew from his personal pension plan. The company was on COD with 80% of its suppliers, and collection of accounts receivable was very slow, with more than 10% over 120 days past due. The company coffers were nearly empty.

Her first thought was for the employees, many of them loyal workers who'd been on the job for over 15 years. Could she keep them employed? Sarah didn't even know if the company could meet its payroll for the next two weeks. Estate taxes were sure to take a big bite from the estate, and there weren't any liquid assets to pay them with. If she didn't lose the company through bankruptcy, she'd lose it in a fire sale to pay Uncle Sam.

Sarah sat behind her father's desk and wished she were any-where else in the world.

## THE IMPORTANCE OF HAVING A SUCCESSION PLAN

Your company in tatters or sold off to pay estate taxes. Your employ-ees out on the street. Your children feuding with one another. You might think these scenarios are drastic and unusual, but in fact they're more often the rule than the exception. There are over two million entrepreneurial family-owned businesses in the United States that have annual revenues in excess of $1 million—but according to ex-perts, only 37% of these companies will survive to be passed on to the next generation. Only 15% will make it to the generation after that.

The reason? Most entrepreneurs don't have a succession plan.

They retire, fall ill, and die without ever picking and grooming a successor. They don't discuss their plans with their families, so their children fight over who gets to run the business. Or it turns out that none of the children want to run the business and the company gets dismantled in a fire sale. Or the entrepreneur picks an heir but fails to prepare him for the job and his employees resent his succession. Or the entrepreneur doesn't prepare the key employees, so the heir is faced with resentment—or, even worse, the defection of essential employees. Sometimes the entrepreneur *does* choose a successor, but doesn't bother to transfer equity while he's alive and well, and the family ends up losing control of the company to outsiders. Or the entrepreneur doesn't do any estate planning, and the business has to be sold off to pay estate taxes.

But it doesn't have to happen that way. The entrepreneur *can* decide ahead of time who he wants his successor to be. He can discuss it with his family members. He can use his authority as a parent to help his family come to terms with his decisions, so that jealousy or disappointment don't dim their feelings of love for one another. He can devise an equity-transfer plan so that his family retains control of the company. He can establish an outside board to mediate any problems that arise. He can plan his estate so that his family ends up with the maximum amount of resources to run the company and there are enough liquid assets to pay any estate taxes.

In other words, the entrepreneur can plan for his succession. A succession plan is as integral a part of the infrastructure of a business as any of the other topics we've covered in this book. Without one, a company jeopardizes its chances of surviving into the next generation.

In this chapter we'll take you through the steps of a succession plan: developing a strategic business plan, identifying and preparing a successor, making the transition, establishing an outside board, and—most important to the long-term survival of your business—communicating with your family. All too often, the lack of family communication leads directly to the least-desired result: sibling feuding and the eventual loss of the business.

That's what happened to Sarah James and her family.

The second-worst day of Sarah James' life came two years after her father's death. Ever since that awful day in her father's office, she'd been battling to bring the company back to life. She'd laid off half the workforce, reduced all expenses, reduced excessive insurance premiums, sublet unused space, gotten back on credit with suppliers, and outsourced the payroll and accounting functions. The company had become a big part of her life and she felt a sense of ownership. After all, she'd been working 80-hour weeks, doing the job of CEO and controller, and taking only a nominal salary to do so. James Electric had a long way to go before it was healthy, but it wasn't at death's door anymore. That was when she told her brothers and sister she wanted to buy the company. A colleague of her brother Donald provided a valuation of the business. It was ten times higher than Sarah knew the ailing company to be worth. They agreed to get a second valuation from an independent expert. This number was a lot closer to what Sarah thought realistic.

But her siblings didn't see it that way. They thought she was trying to steal the company from them. "Why should I trust your expert instead of mine?" said her brother Donald. It was as if, once the bigger number had been put into their heads, they couldn't get it out. "You're trying to make money off your own family," said her brother Steve. Sarah felt like she'd been kicked in the stomach. Better to lose the company than to lose her family.

James Electric was her father's legacy. It had paid for the family home and put Sarah and her siblings through college. Paul James had spent a lifetime creating it and although he'd never said what he wanted to happen after his death, she was pretty sure it didn't include the dismantling of the big old neon sign that said "James."

"Let's just sell the company," Sarah told her brothers. Sarah had saved the company. Maybe it wasn't too late to save the family.

## THE RIGHT TIME TO PLAN

When should an entrepreneur think about succession planning?

If your company is valuable and you're mortal, you should start thinking about it right now. We know an estate planner who starts every seminar he gives on this topic as follows: "This is only for those of you who are going to die one day. Everyone else can leave the room."

It's pretty much the same thing with succession planning. Of course, an entrepreneur doesn't launch a company with a fully developed succession plan already in place. However, once the company begins to have any value at all, he should start thinking about how he wants to pass that value on.

Ideally, from that point onward, an entrepreneur should always have two plans for succession: a plan for what happens if he's hit by a bus tomorrow, and a plan for what happens when he retires gracefully at 94.

We have one client, a CEO of a successful $50 million aerospace firm, who at the relatively early age of 60, and in perfect health, came to us to start a succession plan. "I've planned everything else about my business," he said, "and it's always worked for me. Why shouldn't I have a plan for this?" Certainly, with age and with the increased value of a business, the issue of succession planning becomes more pressing. But not everyone sees it that way.

Why? Because no one, no matter how fearless in business, no matter how willing to take risks in the marketplace, no matter how clear-eyed and coolheaded in pursuit of the competitive edge, likes to think about the day he won't be running his own company. We've been amazed over the years at how CEOs who can look down the jaws of economic disaster and emerge triumphant will put off thinking about succession planning.

It's perfectly understandable. For one thing, when an entrepreneur builds up a company over many years, he comes to identify very closely with his creation. He can't imagine the company without him and he can't imagine himself without the company.

For another thing, succession planning often brings up psychologically loaded issues about loved ones and colleagues: the son who wants to take over, but probably doesn't have it in him; the daughter who is actually the most capable but who is more interested in becoming a doctor; the younger wife whose role in the company is deeply resented by her stepchildren; the loyal manager who has worked at the entrepreneur's side for years and believes he is owed an equity position.

Finally, succession planning seems to involve the loss of control. As the CEO of the company, you're the boss. Not only are you used to being in control, but you've been used to it for years. The idea of planning for the time when someone else will be in control can seem very foreign.

However, there is another way to look at all of this.

Succession planning isn't about giving up control; it's about maintaining control and deciding how you pass on your company. Obviously, one way or another, you're going to be giving up your company eventually. Succession planning allows you to control how that happens.

And painful as it may be to contemplate the world without you in it, it would be infinitely more painful to contemplate a world in which your company no longer existed and your family no longer spoke to each other.

While family-related issues can be thorny, they can be handled by learning to wear two hats: the family hat and the business hat. As a father, husband, and friend, your heart often tells you to make decisions that your businessman's head tells you to avoid. If it seems impossible to wear both these hats at once, that is because it *is* impossible. The trick is to wear one hat at a time and to always make it clear which one you've got on.

We know of one CEO who, against his better business judgment, promoted his son Peter to vice president of marketing. The son was a very conservative, detail-oriented type (the exact opposite, in fact, of his father) and within six months he had managed to quash every good idea that came across his desk. Within a year, the marketing division was hemorrhaging employees and morale was dropping precipitously. Much as it pained him as a father, the CEO knew he had to act. He put on his business hat, called Peter into his office, and fired his own son. Then he took off his business hat and put on his family hat. "Peter," he said, "I understand you're out of a job. What can I do to help?"

What makes succession planning daunting is that it is not like other activities that require a transient engagement with one's mortality—such as making a will, buying life insurance, or working with an estate planner. All these tasks can be accomplished relatively quickly, but succession planning is a process that can take years.

In fact, ideally, succession planning, like strategic planning, is a continuous process. Your succession plan can't sit on a shelf, gathering dust. It has to reflect the state of your business, which is constantly changing. As your business changes, so will your succession plan.

## STRATEGIC PLANNING

Succession planning starts with strategic planning. In order to come up with a succession plan that makes sense, you have to know where your company is now, and where you want it to go in the future.

As we discussed in chapter two, the first steps of a strategic plan are the review of your company's internal health and an assessment of market conditions. What you learn from these assessments is crucial to how you plan for succession. Let's take the example of James Electric. When Paul James's daughter Sarah took over the company, she found that sales were declining due to defense cutbacks, expenses were outstripping revenue, insurance costs were way out of line for the company's diminished worth, the payroll was too big, and the traditional market for the company's electronic products—the Defense Department—could no longer be relied upon. A strategic plan assessment would have revealed all this while Paul James was still in charge—and able to do something about it.

In failing health, he might not have tried to fix the company single-handedly. Perhaps he would have decided to sell the business and leave the proceeds to his children. Or perhaps he would have taken one or more of the children into the business with him, so they could start rebuilding the company together. Still another option would have been to bring in outside talent to lead the company in a new direction. The point is, the succession question and the strategic assessment are intertwined.

A strategic plan will also help guide your choice if you have more than one possible heir. For instance, let's say your company used to make computer hardware, but business conditions have recently forced you to shift into software. Instead of a stable, mature company that needs a caretaker, suddenly what you are leaving your children has become a rapidly changing business that needs a CEO with the vision and the moxie to lead it into new territory. Perhaps your restless son, who always seemed bored with the company, will now fit right in. Or perhaps your daughter with years of experience at a staid corporate giant will now no longer be the ideal candidate. As business conditions change, so will your succession plan.

If a strategic plan is a road map of where you want the company to go, a succession plan tells you who is going to guide the company to that destination. It also tells you how to find and prepare that person.

## IDENTIFYING YOUR SUCCESSOR

The successor may be obvious; the entrepreneur may have one child already working in the company, who loves the business and wants to succeed when the entrepreneur is ready to retire. But rarely is it so simple. Perhaps none of your children wants the job; perhaps none of them is an appropriate choice. In these cases, the entrepreneur is forced to look outside the immediate family to a more distant relative, a key employee already in the company, or a hired gun.

Either way, it's important to figure out what kind of qualifications a successor should have. It may seem obvious to say that these qualifications should be worked out in advance, *before* you start considering candidates, but when family members are concerned, it is easy to pick a successor first and then try to justify the decision with qualifications.

If you are considering a family member, this is the time to take off your family hat and put on your business hat. Objectively, what are the qualifications your successor will need to do the job? What kind of education, experience, and temperament are necessary?

One factor that will influence the answer to this question is the state of development of your company. As we said before, a mature company needs a different kind of CEO than does a rapidly expanding start-up. If you live to a ripe old age, and your company grows and matures as you expect, then your young daughter who doesn't like to take risks but who has an incredible head for figures may turn out to be the perfect choice. However, if you have to step down in five years, before the business has a chance to gel, then your entrepreneurial-minded son who risked his entire savings to start a pizza-delivery service when he was in college might be a better choice.

Your children and relatives are your obvious heirs, but they are not the only people who can succeed you. That's what Joe Johnson of Johnson Aerospace decided. He spent 30 years building his $40 million company and he wanted to make sure it stayed in the family. He also wanted to ensure that the Johnson legacy would continue on into the next generation. When men colonize Mars, Joe confidently expects Johnson components to be there.

Joe had three children, one of whom, a son, was already working in the business. His daughter worked for a department store, and his other son was an engineer in a related field. All three were bright, but when Joe thought about succession with his business hat on, he realized that none of his children would be able to lead the company. Instead, he chose Frank Gale, a key employee. In exchange for giving up the possibility of equity at a publicly owned company, Frank would get to play a major role at Johnson Aerospace, bring along future generations of owners, and—since family businesses tend to be more stable than public corporations—he would be relatively safe from the uncertainties of the corporate job market.

Being the non-family manager of a family business is not all wine and roses; there are drawbacks, not the least of which involve dealing with intrafamily squabbles. Johnson realized he would have to come up with a good compensation package to make the job attractive to Frank Gale.

Since many entrepreneurs want to keep the company stock within the family, other means of compensation have to be explored. One popular alternative is a phantom stock plan: If the value of the company increases, the manager gets the increase in the value of a predetermined number of shares of "stock." Another alternative might be deferred compensation or bonuses tied to the performance of the company.

The Johnson children will continue to own Johnson Aerospace, but they will not be running it. Joe Johnson set up a voting trust to oversee the company, gave Frank Gale a generous salary plus phantom stock, and set up trustees to protect his children's interests.

In a voting trust, the ownership stays in the family, but all voting rights go to trustees who are professional trust managers. The trustees have a high level of legal obligation to the beneficiaries and a correspondingly high level of personal liability—if they fail to act in the interests of the beneficiary or beneficiaries, they can be sued.

Once the entrepreneur has chosen a successor, it's important to bring everyone into the loop. Top management should be informed immediately; the choice may engender resentment now, but that is much preferable to resentment later when the entrepreneur is not around to help control it. When succession occurs unexpectedly, without planning and communication, the ascent of an heir can cause jealousy and lead to the loss of key employees at a time when the company cannot afford to lose them. This is especially true if the heir-apparent has not been properly prepared to rule.

## TRAINING A SUCCESSOR

Once you've picked a successor, you have to figure out how to prepare her for the job. In general, there are two places she can get experience: inside your company and outside it.

There are a number of advantages to outside work experience. In someone else's company, she won't have an inside track; she'll have to prove herself on her own merits, which can be a salutary and confidence-building experience. This will also tend to give her more credibility later on when she moves to your company, lessening any potential resentment from her new colleagues and siblings. Another advantage is that it will give her the chance to see how other companies do things, particularly if she can arrange to work for one of your principal competitors.

When you bring the person you're grooming as your successor into the company, she should be brought in at a level commensurate with her experience and training. A good example of tailoring the job to the child's experience is what Samuel Tilly did at Tilly Tiles, a $40 million bathroom tile company. Samuel had three children who he wanted to bring into the business. They had extremely disparate backgrounds. His eldest son had just earned an MBA from Harvard. His younger son had joined the company right out of high school, working his way up from truck driver to floor manager before leaving for a stint in the Green Berets. Now back from the army, he wanted to return to the company. His only daughter had recently graduated college with a bachelor's degree in business.

Sam's problem was how to choose appropriate jobs and fair compensation for his children. The eldest son could easily have parlayed his MBA into a high salary on Wall Street, but Sam never even thought of trying to match a Wall Street salary. It would have created resentment on the part of the other two children.

Sam decided to hire the three children at the same salary—but he gave them jobs that reflected their expertise. The MBA became a vice president responsible for all financial affairs; the ex–Green Beret, always very popular with the employees from his years of working for the company, was made head of operations; and the daughter was put in charge of human resources. Which of the three will take over the family business? Time will tell. In the meantime, Tom is giving invaluable experience to his successor—whoever that might be.

## MAKING THE TRANSITION

Once you've established a succession plan for your company, you also need to establish one for yourself. This is often the hardest part of the succession process because it means letting go of the reins. Most CEOs are not the kind of people who like to loll on the beach. In fact, what often happens in successful transitions is that the CEO develops a strong interest in an area outside the company and ends up working just as hard as he did before. Sometimes it's politics, sometimes it's public service. Sometimes it's a secondary ambition or "ghost" career such as painting or writing. For some particularly ruthless CEOs it's golf. We've known several CEOs who have started entirely new businesses and gone on to build even larger companies in the "twilight" of their careers.

Unfortunately, sometimes the entrepreneur simply can't let go. The succession plan is in place, and so is he—at his desk. Take the Crandall Lumber Company. John Crandall did a lot of things right: He groomed his son, Mack, to take his place, informed his key employees of his plans, and gave Mack the title of CEO. But psychologically, John wasn't able to let go. He kept his old office at the plant, from which he "advised and consulted," forcing his son to check with him on every detail. Why didn't Mack stand up to his father? Because his father still owned the company. John had never transferred equity to his son. Eventually, Mack quit in frustration. His father had given him the title, but had never given up the power.

## EQUITY TRANSFER

Once an entrepreneur has established how power will be transferred, he needs to transfer ownership—which is not necessarily the same thing. We once heard an entrepreneur say to his son, "You have a birthright to *own* this company, but you don't have a birthright to *run* it—you'll have to earn that." In fact, making a clear distinction between who has ownership of the company and who has the power to run it is one of the key aspects of succession planning.

If control of the company is given to a family member, that person must have enough power to be an effective leader. This power can be based on support from an outside board, the entrepreneur's correct positioning of his successor before the succession, or even the personal dynamism of the new CEO, but probably the most effective control is weighted ownership. When each of the family members shares equal ownership, it can be very difficult for one of them to lead effectively. The new CEO tries to assume command, but the other family members (who may feel slighted at having been passed over for the top position) have a tendency to second-guess—and because they own equal amounts of stock, they can bring the company to a standstill.

An example of what can happen when control and ownership are not clearly defined is the situation that developed at Essian Glass and Linen, a $30 million restaurant-supply company. Armand Essian, the owner and entrepreneur who founded the company, was a human dynamo who did the work of five men. Armand assumed he would live forever, so when he died suddenly of a heart attack at 58, there was no succession plan in place. In his will, he had left the ownership of the company equally to the members of his immediate family: his wife, two sons, and two daughters. However, there were no instructions as to who would run the business.

None of the children had any experience in the business, but the youngest daughter, Lilly, volunteered to take over, quitting her job at a not-for-profit health-care company. Lilly was a quick study and managed to increase revenues modestly, but her siblings were not impressed—and since they sat on the company's board, that became a problem. They began to question Lilly's competence and authority; after all, as they said to her, she didn't have any more experience than they did. "What gives you the right," one brother asked, "to make decisions that affect us?" Lilly found herself wasting hours at board meetings to justify even her minor decisions. In one case, the family called a board meeting to discuss her plan to buy a forklift. When it came to major issues about the company's future, the conflicts between Lilly and her siblings were even worse: Lilly wanted to reinvest profits and grow the business; her siblings wanted to maximize their dividends.

Clearly, this all could have been avoided. If Armand Essian had discussed his succession with his family, he might have learned that Lilly was interested in taking over. Through family discussions, Armand could have empowered Lilly in the eyes of her siblings. He could have brought her into the company earlier to learn the business, helping to ensure the economic stability of the company. He could have devised an equity-transfer plan that divided ownership equally but gave Lilly exclusive control. Or, he could have given Lilly a larger share of the stock in the company and made up the difference to his wife and the other siblings by giving them other assets.

## ESTABLISHING AN OUTSIDE BOARD

There was one other thing Armand Essian could have done to ensure the future safety of his company: He could have set up an outside board to help referee family differences after he was gone.

As we will discuss in chapter eight, setting up an outside board would be a good idea even if an entrepreneur were going to live forever. Board members can supply expertise in areas with which the CEO is unfamiliar, as well as provide an arena for the CEO to discuss broad policy decisions. An outside board can also be helpful to the entrepreneur in the midst of succession planning. Board members who are not embroiled in family issues are often able to bring clarity to muddled situations and give dispassionate advice to the entrepreneur.

But if an outside board is helpful for the first generation, it can be absolutely critical for the second. All too often, siblings who have grown up together have trouble dealing with each other in a respectful and professional way. If the outside board is made up of people of appropriate experience, it will have credibility with *all* of the family members—and keep board meetings from descending into petty family squabbles, or worse, family brawls.

A qualified outside board is usually welcomed by family members, who are often relieved to have someone outside the family to whom they can appeal. Board members have the advantage of being both intimately involved in the affairs of the company and above the fray at the same time.

A new CEO can use the board as a counterweight to uninformed ideas and suggestions from family members who are not actively involved in running the business. The board can also help with questions about how the CEO is compensated. This issue is often a lightning rod for jealousy, resentment, and ill will. Siblings who are not involved typically feel that the sibling who is in charge has a cushy job and is getting too much money. The compensation committee of the board can help to alleviate those feelings.

## FAMILY COMMUNICATION

Succession planning is one of the most important things an entrepreneur can do to ensure the continued survival of his company. However, without continued family communication throughout the planning process and beyond, there is the real possibility that the company may not survive.

If the entrepreneur has not communicated his wishes for the business while he is still around to explain himself, misunderstandings and hurt feelings can tear a family apart later. Sometimes the entrepreneur keeps quiet out of a misguided sense of tact or a desire to avoid an unpleasant scene. However, if there's bad news for a family member, it is much better that he hear it from the entrepreneur in person, not at the reading of the will.

The best policy is to be open and frank. We spoke earlier of the family hat versus the business hat. It is possible to wear both, but not simultaneously. If an entrepreneur has brought his children into the business, it is important to establish criteria for what they have to do in order to succeed. And it is equally important that they receive frequent feedback. Informal meetings on a regular basis are a wonderful first step, but we have also found it beneficial to establish an annual family meeting, separate from the board meeting. Here, the entrepreneur can give and get feedback and provide updates on the company's strategic plan, on his succession plan and estate plan, and on the transfer of equity. It is also here that the entrepreneur can make his case for his vision of the company's future.

If the infrastructure of a company is the hidden fabric that holds it together, then succession planning must be considered a vital part of any business infrastructure. A company without the sense of continuity that comes from knowing that the future has been planned for is a company that may have no future.

## ENTREPRENEUR'S SUMMARY

Of the more than two million entrepreneurial family owned businesses in the United States, only 37% will survive to be passed on to the next generation. Only 15% will make it to the generation after that. The primary reason for this is the lack of a plan for succession.

A succession plan is as integral a part of the infrastructure of a business as any of the other topics we've covered in this book. Without one, a company jeopardizes its chances of surviving into the next generation.

There are five essential ingredients to any succession plan:

1. *Developing a strategic business plan.* A review of your company's internal health and an assessment of market conditions—the beginning steps of strategic planning—are crucial to how you plan for succession. If the company you are leav-

ing behind is mature and stable, it will need a different kind of successor at the helm than if it is a new start-up. And the succession plan that you decide on today may have to be altered as business conditions change.

2. *Identifying and preparing a successor.* When family members are concerned, it is easy to pick a successor first and then try to justify the decision with qualifications. However, these qualifications should be worked out in advance, *before* you start considering candidates.

   Your children and relatives are your obvious candidates, but they are not the only people who can succeed you. When the decision is made, top management should be informed immediately; the choice may engender resentment now, but that is much preferable to resentment later, when the entrepreneur is not around to help control it.

3. *Making the transition.* The hardest part of the succession process is letting go of the reins. If you continue to stay involved in the day-to-day operations, your successor will not get the credibility and respect he needs to succeed. In addition to handing over management control, it is also important to transfer ownership.

4. *Establishing an outside board.* If an outside board is helpful for the first generation, it can be absolutely critical for the second. A board of directors can give an objective viewpoint that may help to prevent a family from falling apart.

5. *Communicating with your family.* If the entrepreneur has not communicated his wishes for the business while he is still around to explain himself, misunderstandings and hurt feelings can tear a family apart later.

   In making these decisions, an entrepreneur must wear two hats: the family hat and the business hat. It is possible to wear both, but not simultaneously. If an entrepreneur has brought his children into the business, it is important to establish criteria for what they have to do in order to succeed. And it is equally important that they receive frequent feedback.

# Finding and Retaining Good People

What does an entrepreneur need to grow his company?

A vision for the future—and the infrastructure to accomplish it. An information system that's accurate and timely—and the technology to achieve it. A succession plan to protect and continue his legacy.

All these things are essential, but they don't mean much without the right people. People with creativity, energy, and skills. People who can understand the entrepreneur's goals and run with the ball. People who can document and order their work without stifling their creativity. That's what this chapter is about: finding those people, retaining them, and compensating them appropriately.

## THE CHALLENGE OF THE ENTREPRENEURIAL COMPANY

Hiring the right people presents special challenges for the entrepreneurial company. While a mature company is likely to have established recruitment and hiring methods, the entrepreneurial company may have to "invent" its hiring and recruitment processes as it goes along. Because the entrepreneurial company grows and changes dramatically, it's not only filling jobs, but creating positions that didn't previously exist. In contrast, when a mature company has to make a hire, the job has probably existed for some time; a number of people have filled it; over the years, managers have discovered what kinds of people work well in that job; and there's probably a clear-cut job description attached to the position.

But let's see what happens when a fast growing entrepreneurial company decides to make a hire. Mighty Manufactures, a Midwestern manufacturing firm, was started five years ago by Ben Hadley and Jack Deligter. Ben handled operations and production and Jack was in charge of administration and sales. For the first five years, their two-man management team ran the entire company so effectively that they reached annual revenues of $25 million. However, with large new contracts in the offing, they decided to add several new people to their management team, including a CFO, a marketing person, and an information systems manager.

Since none of these positions had ever existed at the company before, this presented challenges both for Ben and Jack and for the people they were going to hire. For the prospective employees, the challenge was in taking on jobs that had not yet been defined and against which there were no benchmarks to measure their perform-ances. For Ben and Jack, there was the prospect of giving up some control and responsibility. Most importantly, they had to choose man-agers who would fit into a company structure that had yet to be invented. 

How do you find someone to fit a job when you're not exactly sure what the shape of the job is? *By understanding what you need a potential employee to do.*

## DEFINING YOUR NEEDS

Since a new job doesn't have a fixed structure and shape, the entrepre-neurial employer can't fall back on a well-established job description. He has to invent one. What is the purpose of this job? Why does this position exist? Employers need to know four things about the job they're offering:

1. Its role in achieving the company's strategic goals

2. The key responsibilities of the job

3. The knowledge, skills, and abilities necessary to do the job

4. What type of training and development the employer will provide to the employee

Ben and Jack may never have employed a CIO before, but there are important things they already know about the job. They know they need someone to bring their information system into sync with the growing needs of their company. The job, then, requires figuring out what kind of system the company needs, costing it out, obtaining it and implementing it, providing for training, troubleshooting any problems, and then using it creatively to provide the company with information and new opportunities. Thus, the job has aspects of research, technological literacy, education, budgeting, troubleshooting, analytic thinking, and project management.

Based on how they've defined the job, Ben and Jack also know a lot about what they're looking for in a candidate. The candidate has to be completely familiar and comfortable with technologies and both the operational and accounting functions. But he can't be just a technician; he has to be creative—after all, he's creating a system—but he also has to be orderly because the system he creates must be accurate and reliable. He needs to be a self-starter, comfortable with creating structure rather than someone who needs structure. He has to be able to communicate well with his peers. He also has to communicate well upwards (with Ben and Jack) and downwards (the employees who have to be educated in the use of the new system). He has to be able to create and adhere to a budget. And he has to be someone who can work on his own without guidance or supervision, because although Ben and Jack will approve the big decisions, they don't want to get bogged down in the details.

There are advantages to creating a new position. The lack of a job description can be liberating. Traditional job descriptions often leave little "wiggle room." These days, the duties of an employee can change very rapidly; job descriptions tend to lag behind. As we mentioned in our chapter on "Building Your Team," defining roles is more important than defining specific duties. In fact, a list of key job responsibilities shouldn't number more than eight; any more and the chances are a job description has been created that may prove too rigid.

Because the jobs it has to offer tend to be general and open to definition, an entrepreneurial company has to pay a lot of attention to the skills, talents, and past performance of candidates seeking those jobs. And regardless of the position, certain kinds of abilities are desirable to the entrepreneurial company.

## CREATIVITY VS. STRUCTURE

An entrepreneur needs people who are skilled at developing processes as well as maintaining them: creative people, who can solve problems, think in a nontraditional way, and who don't need direction. On the other hand, employees who work entirely on their own, never document what they're doing, and can't work within any structure won't be of much use to the company. Keeping a balance between creativity and orderliness is one of the big challenges facing any entrepreneurial company.

The temptation for the entrepreneur is to either hire someone exactly like himself ("We need more people like me") or exactly his opposite ("We need someone to keep me grounded"). Neither is a good idea.

If the entrepreneur hires his complete opposite to generate discipline, he may stifle creativity and the relationship will likely be difficult. That's what happened at Teach Technology, a manufacturer of educational software. The founders were two young women who had an idea every other minute. To impose order on their creative chaos, they hired their exact opposite, a CFO with the mentality of a detail-oriented bookkeeper. And of course, the CFO drove them crazy. He said "no" to everything and everyone because he was focusing only on the numbers, not on the strategic goals of the company. The CFO kept telling people why they couldn't do the things they wanted to do—start a campaign in a new market, hire a new engineer for product development, buy a new computer system—instead of helping them to figure out how to do things that made business sense. He had a short-time reference and couldn't see the larger picture. Teach Technology eventually brought in a new CFO who still says "no" when necessary, but who can see the future and who is as committed to growing the company as its two founders.

Entrepreneurs also run into problems when they hire in their own image. A whole management team of creative, independent, let-the-paperwork-fall-where-it-may employees is going too far in the other direction. That's what Bob and Jack ended up with at Midwestern Manufactures. None of their strategic plans—a new marketing campaign, an information system—were making progress because the members of the new management team were going off in different directions. Where their jobs overlapped, each wanted to proceed in his own way. Ideally, an entrepreneurial company needs individuals who balance creativity with orderliness, nontraditional thinking with a respect for the rules.

Naturally, this is exactly what most job candidates say they offer. But how can you tell if someone really has those qualities?

## INTERVIEW TECHNIQUES

There's no magic formula to interviewing; in fact, most successful interviewers say that, ultimately, they have to rely on their intuition. However, there are some techniques that can be helpful.

One clue to the job-seeker's suitability is his employment pattern. Has he taken jobs with an element of risk before? If not, he may be ill-suited to the uncertainties of life at an entrepreneurial firm. On the other hand, if he's held positions that didn't exist before his tenure, that's a pretty good sign that he may have the initiative and energy it takes to work in an entrepreneurial company. Sometimes such a person will have been hired by small- and medium-sized companies to create a new position. Perhaps he began a project and then moved on, once the job had become routine. This kind of pattern doesn't necessarily mean instability or lack of loyalty; it can mean the person enjoys challenges. On the other hand, a lot of job-hopping for which a candidate cannot supply an explanation can be a danger signal.

For that matter, any question for which a candidate cannot supply an explanation is reason for caution. Are there unexplained gaps in his resume? Is his resume missing dates? Is he vague, either in person or on paper, about what his job duties were or why he left a job? Does he fail to answer questions directly? Is he reluctant to give specifics?

Jobs with entrepreneurial companies sound fun and exciting, and many people apply who don't have the necessary kind of temperament. They may be risk-averse, or they may be unable to work well without a lot of structure. If such a person presents himself well, this can be quite difficult to spot.

That's how Bob Billings got his job at Travis Housewares. You remember Travis Housewares—the firm headed up by the brilliant but erratic Charles Travis. Billings was the third person to be hired as CFO in five years. Travis couldn't keep anyone in the job because he kept interfering with the CFO's autonomy. By the time Billings was hired, however, Travis, as part of his succession plan, had brought his son Ken into the business.

Ken was determined to find and keep the right CFO. At the interview, Billings seemed to be that person. He'd held a similar position at another company of the same size, he was a qualified CPA, he was excited about the potential of Travis Housewares, and he described himself as a "problem-solver and self-starter."

As it turned out, Billings was anything but. He was good at coordinating but lacked the initiative to lead a department. His inability to take the initiative extended to even simple problems. For instance, Billings's department had a serious computer and filing cabinet shortage. The lack of computers made it difficult to handle the daily workload and the overstuffed files were a constant irritant. Desks overflowed with piles of files for which there were no cabinets. Billings complained about the situation in his first month at the company. Travis's son, Ken, immediately authorized Billings to buy what he needed.

A month went by. Nothing happened. Ken reminded Billings that he had been given permission to make the purchases. Billings said he was looking into it. Another month went by, and Ken reminded him again. Billings said he was still working on it.

Billings was far from the self-starter he had claimed to be. Did he lie to get the job? Probably not. He just didn't know what he was suited for—which makes it all the more important that the entrepreneur screen candidates as thoroughly as possible.

Some of what an entrepreneur wants to find out in an interview—a candidate's skills, education, job background— can be determined through straightforward questioning. But not everything can be. Most people are like Bob Billings; when asked if they're creative problem-solvers, they look you straight in the eye and say, "Yes."

Some interviewers attempt to find out how someone handles problems by asking the candidate about a major challenge he faced or problem he solved. However, most candidates come prepared for that question and so their answers are rarely revealing. A better approach is to ask him to describe how he handled a situation in his old job that is similar to the one he will find in his new job with you. If a candidate can't tell you true stories about his experience with a satisfactory level of detail, he may simply not have the level of experience you're looking for.

## INTERVIEW ETIQUETTE

Interview etiquette is usually discussed from the applicant's point of view—being polite, on time, professional. However, interview etiquette goes both ways. Applicants have a right to expect professionalism, courtesy, and, above all, confidentiality. If a person is already employed, the utmost tact and sensitivity have to be exercised when making contact. It's a good idea not to take anything for granted. The employer should make and observe agreements with the candidate about where, when, and how it's appropriate to make contact.

We know one entrepreneur of a small, dynamic start-up manufacturing company who was looking for someone to spearhead the company's marketing department. The human resources person set up an initial interview with a top marketing person working for a direct competitor. The interview went very well—so well that three hours after the interview, the entrepreneur, a very decisive woman, decided to hire the candidate. She called and left a message on his office voice mail. Unfortunately, his secretary picked up the message and mentioned it to the CFO's secretary, who mentioned it to the CEO's secretary . . .

That said, however, most professional recruiters and human resource people are very discreet, so if a candidate has been reassured about confidentiality but continues to withhold basic information such as the name of her current employer or dates of employment, it should raise serious questions. And needless to say, a candidate who lies is no longer a candidate.

Once a candidate is a serious contender for the job, references should be checked. In addition to verifying the basics, there are two purposes the entrepreneur accomplishes by a reference check: (1) validating what he thinks he already knows about a serious candidate; and (2) learning information that will help him get the new relationship off to a good start.

A reference check should not be an attempt to "get the dirt" on a prospective employee. If he's gotten this far in your screening process, then you are already satisfied that he is a satisfactory candidate. Many employers today are reluctant to give employment histories, because of legal implications. The following approach is a guideline for a reference check:

> We are seriously considering hiring X. We want the relationship to be successful. We understand this person's strengths and weaknesses and we'd like your input on what we can provide to this person in terms of support, direction, and skill development.

If the query is handled in a positive and ethical way, most former employers will feel comfortable responding.

With increased awareness of, and concern for, legal liability, many companies are becoming leery of supplying employment references—both negative and positive. If you are not able to get information about a candidate, do not assume the reference is poor or hold it against the candidate. Go with the information you have and make your own decision.

Given the current legal climate, it's vitally important that you comply with the employment laws regarding interviewing, selection, promotion, and compensation. There are employment law seminars which can provide guidance in this area, and of course it's always wise to consult with your legal advisors.

There's one last thing to look for when hiring someone: Not only should the prospective employee's skills fit the job, but her values should also fit the employer's values. By values, we don't mean that the employer and employee must vote the same way or watch the same sit-coms, but it is vital that the employer have a clear and consistent vision of the philosophy of the job—and that the prospective employee should share that vision. If employer's and employee's understanding of the work ethic or principles of making business decisions diverge too radically, it will lead to an ultimately unproductive working relationship.

Let's say an employer is interviewing a marketing candidate. The employer believes that the only thing that matters is making a sale. During the interview, it becomes clear that the prospective employee doesn't want to sell anything he doesn't believe is valuable. That's the kind of conflict that isn't going to go away. Another example of a basic value conflict is the long-term investment-motivated entrepreneur and the short-term cash-motivated CFO. Sometimes entrepreneurs think that a conflict in core values doesn't matter because they have the final word. But in our experience, it does matter. If you like everything about a candidate except his core values, keep looking.

## RECRUITING

The obvious ways to find employees are classified ads and professional recruiters. These methods certainly have their place, but the obvious isn't always the best.

One of the entrepreneur's most valuable recruiting resources is right under his nose: his work force. If employees enjoy working at the company, they are generally eager to make recommendations, and they'll be careful about who they recommend because they're going to have to work with them. To encourage staff recommendations, referral bonuses can be given for hard-to-fill positions. Compared to recruiter's fees, referral bonuses are a bargain.

Financial bonuses are not the only way to generate recommendations from employees. Other rewards work well too: a dinner, a day off, a public thank you, or a letter of appreciation.

In fact, there are a lot of highly qualified people with the right background who will never turn up in response to an ad or a recruiter. That's because they already have jobs—working for the competition. But just because they have jobs now doesn't mean that the entrepreneurial company shouldn't get to know them. For that matter, the entrepreneur doesn't necessarily need to have a position open to be recruiting or conducting informal interviews.

This kind of mutual exploration is known as informational interviewing. It's not about filling specific positions but rather about getting to know the talent pool—before there's a job to fill. Informational interviewing is low-key and low-pressure; the employer is not trying to sell a particular job and the prospective employee is not actively trying to sell himself. Prospective employees get a chance to talk about what they do and the entrepreneur can tell them about his company. This can actually be fun for both sides. In effect, the entrepreneur is saying, "This is mine. This is what I've built, and I want to show it to you." The employee is saying, "This is who I am. This is what I've attained."

If an entrepreneur has been conducting informal informational interviews over the months, then when he does have a job to fill, he'll have a list of potential candidates who he's met and liked. By then, those people may still be working elsewhere and uninterested in moving, or they may be ready and eager to make a move, or they may know of someone who might be a potential candidate. The major thing to keep in mind is that the entrepreneur and his management team need to be out in the market, looking for new talent all the time. When doing this kind of interviewing, the entrepreneur should never say that he has a specific job in mind. Instead he should say something like, "I don't have anything specific open right now, but I'm interested in you and I'd like to keep you in mind."

Over time, you get to know people this way. You can keep abreast of where their careers are going and of who's acquiring new skills or experience that is potentially appealing to your company. And by taking a sincere interest in a prospective employee, you begin to build a relationship that will function both as an incentive for him to join the company and as a head start to a cordial working alliance.

It is not unethical to recruit employees from your competitors so long as your motivation is positive: to build your own company as opposed to beating down your competition. It is important however, to remember that roles and relationships change. A prospective employee may be a direct rival later on— or a customer. So it's essential to respect the confidentiality of the interviewing process and to behave professionally at all times. By taking a sincere interest in the progress of the careers of the people you stay in touch with this way, you'll be building goodwill for your company. You'll also be creating more awareness of your company and product.

Another less obvious way to find new talent is through networking. A company's bank, law firm, accountants, the professional-services firms it has, or the relevant trade associations are all possible sources of referrals.

## WHEN BAD HIRES HAPPEN TO GOOD ENTREPRENEURS

The fourth time Ken Travis, the boss' son, found himself reminding Bob Billings, the chief financial officer, to buy new computers and file cabinets, he realized something was seriously amiss. The delay in making these purchases—by itself a rather trivial matter—began to seem symptomatic of a general lack of initiative and leadership. At the first of several meetings, Ken gave the CFO some feedback. The meetings didn't seem to make a difference in Billing's performance, so he was put on six months probation, and finally terminated. The whole process, from the first stirrings of dissatisfaction to the final dismissal, took a year.

Bad hires are expensive—not just in terms of money but in terms of wasted time, effort, and energy. A rapidly expanding entrepreneurial company is particularly vulnerable because of the continual need to fill newly created positions. However, the worst thing the entrepreneur can do is make fast hiring decisions.

It's better to let a position go unfilled until you find the right person than to hire the wrong person to fill it. Not only will you eventually end up firing this wrong person, but you will have spent a lot of resources trying to make it work before you do so. Furthermore, if you have the wrong person in the job for a year, you will be one year further behind your goals for the company. If you are not sure a candidate is the right person, consider hiring him as a consultant or a contract employee.

The use of contract employees is becoming increasingly popular in American business because many businesses feel they can save money on employee benefits. Good reasons for hiring contractors might be because the work is temporary or specialized or because the right permanent person hasn't been located yet. Trying to save money on employee benefits is a bad reason—the savings come at a cost. Contract employees will not be committed to the company, they will bill for all the hours they work, and they may not be as willing to put in the extra effort as staff employees, who have a long-term future with the company. You get what you pay for.

After all, we tell clients, you're probably going to spend more time with these people than you do with your family, so it behooves you to choose carefully.

## RETAINING GOOD PEOPLE

It takes a lot of effort to find good people; once found, you certainly don't want to lose them. But how do you retain good people? The key is to understand their motivations. The idea that money is the main, if not the only, factor motivating employees is a myth. In fact, money is often the least important motivator. Employees may take jobs to make money, but that's not why they stay in them.

That's why entrepreneurs can end up throwing cash around and still lose people. Take what happened at Bradley Investments, a financial-services company run by Nathan Bradley. Nathan Bradley's ambition was to someday make the Forbes list of the Richest Men in America. He loved to work and regularly put in 90-hour weeks. But Nathan made a common and very human error: He assumed his employees were motivated by the same things that motivated him. He worked his brokers and financial analysts hard but paid them well and gave them generous bonuses.

And they all kept leaving. Why? Because the pace was killing them, and Bradley never said "Thank you." It wasn't that Bradley was a rude person; it just never occurred to him to reward with recognition and appreciation. After all, *he* wasn't working for thank you's.

The best way to find out what motivates employees is to ask them. People are driven by many different things: money, security, the emotional rewards of recognition, the promise of promotion, the satisfaction of doing a good job and working to their full potential. Generally, however, it comes down to some combination of appreciation, financial reward, opportunity, and challenge.

## LET THEM DO THEIR JOB

Entrepreneurial companies tend to be exciting and challenging environments. So how does it happen that creative employees end up doing boring work? Because sometimes entrepreneurs hire independent people and then proceed to tell them exactly what to do.

Interfering with the responsibilities and authority of managers is a surefire method of losing them. For instance, although Bob Billings was fired for incompetence, the two people who preceded him in the position of CFO of Travis Housewares left on their own. The reason? They were never given any autonomy. It wasn't just that Charles Travis wouldn't let them visit the factories or talk to the banks; he told them what color binder to use for their financial reports.

But entrepreneurial interference isn't always the result of an inability to share power. Remember Ben Hadley and Jack Deligter? They went from a partnership to a management team almost overnight. Ben and Jack had the best intentions in the world. They sought and hired really smart, aggressive, independent people. But the team came in without any infrastructure in place—and very soon, there was chaos. Five months after he was hired, the CIO still hadn't made any visible progress in getting an information system in place.

"I'm waiting for the CFO to tell me how much I can spend," the CIO explained.

"I can't budget this until I get a report about the options," said the CFO.

Jack and Ben were disgusted. "Maybe we should just do this ourselves," said Ben.

"No," said Jack. "We hired them it's our responsibility to tell them what to do."

In our experience, both these solutions result in disaster. The former results in the inability to delegate that we've discussed in other chapters; the latter results in micromanagement. The right approach is neither to micromanage nor to assume all the responsibility. The right approach is to lead. Leadership means that the entrepreneur states the goals—where he wants to go—and his managers figure out how to accomplish those goals—how they're going to get there.

This is what Ben and Jack ultimately did.

"We want to see a report with budgeted options by the end of the month," they said at the next meeting. "We don't care how it gets done. And another thing: Both of you are responsible for it being on our desk."

Naturally, it was.


## RECOGNITION AND APPROPRIATE REWARDS

Pizza parties. Muffin carts. Company pens. Clowns at the company picnic. These are all things that employers resort to in an effort to motivate their employees and keep them happy. There are two fallacies here. The first fallacy is that creating happy employees is an appropriate goal for an employer. It is not. An employer's goal is to run a successful business and to give employees an opportunity to contribute to and share in that success while developing their own skills. If this happens, it will result in job satisfaction for his employees. The role of a business leader and manager is to facilitate the on-the-job success of employees. Job satisfaction comes from job success.

The second fallacy is that people work for pizza. In point of fact, they work for challenge, opportunity, recognition, and the potential for better pay or advancement. A happy work environment is very important, but a truly happy work environment is a result of personnel feeling that they have been challenged, recognized, and rewarded. Pizza and company pens can play a part in this, of course, but they cannot take the place of daily recognition by a supervisor or of the opportunity for promotion and a raise.

A cautionary word needs to be said about promotions. Promotions are business decisions, not rewards. Employees should be promoted based on the requirements of the job to which they are being promoted, not the requirements or the performance of their previous job. Their previous job, however well they've been performing it, may require completely different skills. In other words, the criteria for promotions should be anticipated performance in the new job, not past performance in the old job. Otherwise, entrepreneurs risk enacting the Peter Principle: promoting people past their level of competence.

Sometimes the guiltiest practitioners of the Peter Principle are the nicest people. We're thinking of one small family firm in particular: the Culbertsons. Nina and Harvey Culbertson inherited Culbertson Carts from their father, who started the grocery and shopping cart company after World War II. Nina and Harvey inherited a workforce with a lot of years on the job and with the atmosphere of an extended family. Of course, Nina and Harvey wanted to make a profit, but they also wanted to make sure their employees were treated right. When three of the factory foremen retired, they threw a big party and announced they were promoting three senior tool-and-die makers. These three men were long-term loyal employees and excellent at their jobs. Unfortunately, neither their loyalty nor their technical skills had anything to do with their ability to supervise people.

The three promoted foremen yelled at, criticized, insulted, and regularly terrorized the employees under them. Nina and Harvey felt it would be unseemly to demote such old and valued employees. Meanwhile, morale sank and productivity went down. It's a classic case of why promotion as a reward can be a bad idea.

## REWARDING GOOD PEOPLE: COMPENSATION

The Culbertsons had another problem. Every Christmas, they gave their employees a bonus, and each Christmas, the bonus was a little fatter than the year before. Over time, the employees became so accustomed to it that they planned their mortgages, tuition payments, car loans, etc., around this bonus—as if it were part of their salary. Then, business took a downturn.

After several years of low sales, Nina and Harvey finally tied bonuses to productivity—a rational move that understandably infuriated their employees, who had become so used to the bonuses that they had ceased to be a real reward. What started out as a generous way to thank workers during a period of prosperity had become an entitlement.

When you structure bonuses so that employees come to expect them, you are setting up a situation that is bound at some point to be incompatible with your business goal—which, presumably, is to make a profit. Small, family-owned companies with a paternalistic culture very frequently fall prey to this mistake.

Bonuses not tied to business results are just one example of how good intentions can backfire when it comes to employee compensation. Naturally, we are not advocating stinginess. In fact, appropriate compensation starts with a package of salary, benefits, and incentive pay that is at market value or better.

Some entrepreneurs think they are saving money when they hire cheaply, but it's a false savings—they're getting people from the shallow end of the talent pool. Entrepreneurial companies need people who are *more* qualified than their rivals, not less. If a job candidate is willing to work for less money, it may be because he lacks talent. And even if he has talent and merely lacks experience or self-esteem, this will still impair his ability to function at the highest level. An inexperienced manager is going to spend his time mastering the fundamentals, rather than innovating. An insecure manager may not have the confidence to take risks.

To be competitive, pay within 10% above or below the market average. If the base pay is less than the market average, other aspects of the package should be emphasized to make up for that. Additionally, in today's employment market, a package must include health insurance and some kind of retirement savings plan.

Other elements of a compensation package can include various kinds of deferred compensation such as stock, stock options, stock appreciation rights, phantom stock, and bonuses. But if the cash—i.e., the salary—is lower than what's being offered by other employers, the overall package has to be more attractive. It's just common sense: Cash is always going to be more appealing than other compensation elements.

Setting up a package that emphasizes deferred compensation or incentive pay allows cash-poor companies to compete for good people. But deferred compensation makes good business sense for all companies. A base salary commits a company to paying out a certain amount of cash, regardless of business success, whereas incentive pay or deferred compensation can be tied to results.

The key to incentive pay is that it be offered for specific goals and measurable value. Incentive pay is only appropriate when employee performance can be adequately measured and a monetary value can be assigned to that measure. The performance measures should be very specific and may include any or all of the following: financial, quality, quantity, productivity, and innovation measures.

Measuring performance is easier in some jobs than others. Sales, for instance. The employer promises a bonus for sales over a certain figure; if the salesman makes that many sales, the company pays the salesman a bonus. In other jobs, it's more difficult to measure performance—but more difficult doesn't mean impossible. Customer service, for example, can be measured by level of accuracy or performance to requirements, by the results of customer satisfaction surveys, by repurchase and resell figures, and by complaints.

When incentive pay is set up properly, the employee can say, "I can see from my incentive pay which of my actions has given what kind of value to the company." If that sentence breaks down anywhere—if there's confusion about what the employee is getting rewarded for, or what the measurable value of his actions are to the company, or how his incentive pay reflects that—then the incentive may not be effective.

It usually isn't a good idea to tie incentives to stock prices because most of the time the stock price will reflect more factors than just an employee's performance. Or, to use another example, a firm that sells tractors will be to some extent at the mercy of the commodity markets.

Rewarding or punishing employees based on numbers over which they have no control doesn't make any sense.

For this reason, incentive pay should be self-funded and the company budget should reflect that by setting some money aside in a reserve fund for that purpose. Incentives should be structured so some money always remains in the fund. An employee who's earned his incentive pay shouldn't be penalized because the company, overall, lost money or is having problems. On the other hand, the company shouldn't be spending money it doesn't have. If some money is always kept in the fund, the company and the employees are protected.

Another element of a compensation package is a retirement savings plan. Employees expect and deserve the opportunity to save for retirement. Nowadays that usually means 401(k) plans, which happily do not cost an employer very much. Nowadays, too, it makes more sense to put money into performance vehicles than into retirement vehicles. Traditional fully funded pension plans reward long-term loyalty, but for most employees today, who expect to move several times during a career, they don't offer an incentive.

Furthermore, traditional pensions can have unintended consequences. First of all, they tend to discourage innovation and growth. An employee's goal can become to stay on the job to earn his pension, so he keeps his head down and doesn't take chances.

Second, pension plans that are meant to encourage long-term loyalty can sometimes do the opposite. Employers who offer fully funded pension plans as an incentive to loyalty need to look at the vesting structure of their plans. If, for instance, employees fully vest after five years, it may encourage them to cash out early instead of staying long-term.

## THE LEGAL ISSUES OF EMPLOYMENT

The days when "an honest day's wages for an honest day's work" completely described the contract between employer and employee are long past. Today, an entrepreneur faces complex issues involving the documentation of employment policies and practices, the hiring of employees, the termination of employees, and buy-sell agreements. While a complete discussion of these topics is beyond the scope of this book, we have included in the appendix a sample employee manual which addresses many of these concerns. (See Appendix A: Establishing Effective Employment.)

A new entrepreneurial company may not have had to think about the legal ramifications of employment, but the documentation of company hiring policies and practices is as essential a part of a company's infrastructure as its information systems. Of course, the frequency with which a company will need to consult its lawyers about employment situations can be greatly reduced by making smart hires in the first place.

## GOOD HIRES ARE GOOD BUSINESS

The process by which a growing company *finds* its employees: defining job skills needed well in advance of hiring, acknowledging the need for innovative self-starters who can think for themselves, letting those people do their jobs unhindered, and recruiting in unconventional places.

The process by which a growing company *retains* those employees: motivating through a combination of appreciation, financial reward, opportunity, and challenge.

These processes are the hallmark of a successful employer-employee relationship, and will go a long way toward ensuring the long-term health of any entrepreneurial organization.

## ENTREPRENEUR'S SUMMARY

Hiring the right people presents special challenges for the entrepreneurial company. Because an entrepreneurial company is growing and changing dramatically, it is not only filling jobs but is creating positions that didn't previously exist. In order to make effective hires, an entrepreneur must consider a number of issues:

1. Employers need to know four things about the job they're offering: (i) its role in achieving the company's strategic goals; (ii) the key responsibilities of the job; (iii) the knowledge, skills, and abilities necessary to do the job; and (iv) what type of training and development the employer will provide to the employee.

2. An entrepreneur has to find people who are skilled at developing processes as well as maintaining them: creative people, who can solve problems.

3. Interviewing for an entrepreneurial company involves all the traditional criteria—looking for gaps in the resume, asking candidates to describe how they handled a situation in their old job that is similar to the one they will find in their new job with you, etc.—but also one new criteria: looking for people who have taken jobs with an element of risk before.

4. The traditional methods of seeking out potential employees are fine, but the entrepreneur should also be looking for referrals from his work force and making use of informational interviewing and networking to get to know the talent pool.

5. The key to retaining people is to understand their motivations—and the best way to find out what motivates employees is to ask them. People are driven by many different things: money, security, the emotional rewards of recognition, the promise of promotion, the satisfaction of doing a good job and working to their full potential. The other way to keep good people is to let them do the job you hired them to do. Sometimes entrepreneurs hire independent people and then proceed to tell them exactly what to do, which obviously defeats the purpose of hiring skilled and creative individuals.

6. A truly happy work environment is a result of personnel feeling that they have been challenged, recognized, and rewarded. To be competitive, pay within 10% of the market average. If the base pay is less than the market average, other aspects of the package should be emphasized to make up for that.

   Other elements of a compensation package can include various kinds of deferred compensation such as stock, stock options, stock appreciation rights, phantom stock, and bonuses. The key to incentive pay is that it be tied to specific goals and measurable value.

# Forming a Board of Directors

In the last chapter, we discussed how to develop a management team to help grow an entrepreneurial company. But there is still one important component of the company's team that needs to be addressed: the board of directors.

By law, any incorporated company must have a board of directors. Of course, many entrepreneurs choose to fill these positions with members of management or family who can be counted on to go along with the entrepreneur's decisions. The idea of giving these "directors" any independent oversight function, or of expanding the board to include more members than is required by law, is not tops on the agenda of the heads of most start-ups. Why would an entrepreneur want to have an active and fully functioning board of directors? After all, a board will require meetings, ask questions, generally demand accountability, and distract the management team.

In this chapter, we will tell you why forming a board of directors might just be one of the smartest moves an entrepreneurial company can make, we will explain potential benefits that far outweigh the inconveniences, we will talk about how to go about forming a board, and, finally, we will discuss what its functions ought to be.

## WHY A BOARD?

The general reluctance on the part of entrepreneurs to form an outside board can best be summarized by the reaction of one of our clients, Ted Sommers, when we proposed it to him. His steel company had gone from revenues of $20 million to $100 million in 15 years before hitting the wall. Now, with revenues at $80 million and falling, Ted was seriously worried, and willing to take most suggestions seriously—except this one.

"Are you crazy?" he asked us. "Don't I have enough problems right now without a lot of backseat drivers trying to tell me what to do?"

Of course, the contrarian role *is* one of a board of directors' vital functions. A board exists in part to ask tough questions about management's decisions and strategies. They are there to play devil's advocate—to make sure that a policy has been thought through and that there is some kind of a fallback position if the policy fails.

And yet, a board of directors, properly chosen, can be one of the most positive components of growth a company can have. What are the ways in which a board can round out the management team "package" and add value?

- Board members can offer valuable input and advice. No matter how well rounded an entrepreneur is, there are bound to be areas where he lacks expertise. By choosing board members who fill in the gaps in his own knowledge, he can avoid making costly mistakes. It's a bit like hiring consultants for a tiny fraction of what they would normally charge.

- Board members can act as a sounding board. In their role as monitors of the company, the board may review all major purchases, leases, mergers, and acquisitions. In general, we have found that if your own board can't be convinced that an idea is a good one, then you should go back and get a better idea.

- Board members can provide business contacts and introductions as a company moves into new arenas. When a company decides to manufacture a new product, or expand into a new market, the management team is generally looking for every advantage to make their gamble pay off. Finding the right financing and the right suppliers and distributors, knowing the regulatory aspects of this new market and the mindset of potential new customers—all these things are key. And yet, many companies neglect the easiest and least costly way to acquire this information: through their board of directors. A board comprised of members with diverse talents and backgrounds will have a wide range of contacts that can be of great value to the company.

■ When tough decisions need to be made, the board of directors can take the responsibility and the blame for making them, thus deflecting some of the negative reaction that might otherwise be directed at management. If a senior member of the management team needs to be fired, if a plant needs to be closed, if there can be no dividend distribution this quarter—these are all decisions that can be made by the board.

■ As we have already stated in chapter seven, a board of directors can be very helpful in succession planning. During the planning process, directors can give the entrepreneur plainspoken advice when he is deciding, for example, which of his children is to take over the company. After the transfer of power, a board can help ease the transition by backing the new CEO and keeping board meetings from descending into petty family squabbles.

■ Finally, having a strong board of directors sends a message to the outside world that the company is responsible—which can be particularly valuable when a company needs capital. Obviously, the first things any investor looks at are the numbers: profitability, p/e ratio, the long-term prospects of the business. But the numbers—and, in particular, the projections for the future—are only as good as the managment team that will develop and execute the company's strategy. Investors' comfort levels goes way up when they see familiar faces. Having individuals on your board who are known and respected adds luster to the company. Investors also respect companies with strong management—which is further supported by an independent and strong-minded board of directors.

For all these reasons, an entrepreneur should be giving serious thought to forming a functioning board, even if he is not yet legally obligated to do so.

After all, seen in this light, who *wouldn't* want the advice and support of successful business people with years of experience, hand-picked for their expertise in areas you don't know that much about? Trusted senior advisors who can recommend honest suppliers and expert lawyers; people who can steer you through thickets of regulatory red tape because they've been there before; who can back you up when it comes to a fight; who can take the blame when unpopular decisions have to be made; who can ask the questions that your people, immersed in a situation, might forget to ask?

Our client, Ted Sommers, was pretty sure that he, for one, could resist the siren call of a board of directors. However, with the downturn of his business, he found himself forced into it by his principle bankers. And to his astonishment, he found that the board, instead of meddling and second-guessing, actually helped him to turn the business around.

The first revelation came when he needed a new marketing person. One of his new board members was an acknowledged expert in marketing steel. The director worked with Ted to identify candidates. Together, they found a superb individual who came into the company and turned around the entire function.

But Ted's second revelation was more profound. At first, he had been annoyed by the dislocation within the company every time they had to prepare for a board meeting. The weeks before a meeting were horrible—financial statements had to be brought up to date, executive summaries prepared so the board members could read and understand the issues quickly, new developments had to be analyzed and thought out in preparation for potentially hostile inquiry.

And yet, Ted found that the preparation for these meetings was actually making his company run more smoothly. The process of articulating goals and new directions to interested third parties helped to define and crystalize those goals. The process of preparing ahead of time forced management to meet its deadlines more consistently. The insightful questions that came up in response to presentations sometimes forced management to rethink their plans, and certainly saved them some costly mistakes. The input from the board was invaluable. But in the end, it was their very presence as much as anything they actually said that created a discipline that began to permeate the company.

Ted Sommers is such a believer these days that he has increased the size of his board twice: from five members to seven members, and then from seven members to nine. The last two directors were chosen with an eye toward further expansion. Ted felt he was missing expertise in three key areas. As his company continued to grow, he wanted to be on the cutting edge of management structures and information technology—so he chose as his eighth director an expert in those subjects. He was also taking his company international, and wanted an advisor to guide his path. His ninth director? An individual with years of experience in international business.

## HOW DO YOU FORM A BOARD?

Of course, every company is different and each entrepreneur has to find the mix of backgrounds and personalities, insiders and outsiders, that is right for him and his company. Nonetheless, we've found over the years that there are some guidelines that usually work for most entrepreneurs.

Let's take the question of size first. Except for very large companies, a board should be made up of between 5 and 12 members. A board of more than 12 people is usually too unwieldy; it becomes too difficult to have a discussion in which everyone can be a participant. Conversely, a board with less than 5 members will probably not include a wide enough diversity of experience and contacts to fully benefit the company.

There is widespread agreement in the business community today that independent-minded outside board members without any conflicts of interest best serve an entrepreneur and his company. Accordingly, the current approach is to emphasize the presence of outsiders over insiders. Outside directors by definition do not play a role in the day-to-day management of the company. Inside directors, of course, are employees of the company—generally members of senior management.

Many entrepreneurs are finding that it isn't necessary to have more than one other insider, beside themselves, on the board. An advantage to limiting inside directors is that it cuts down on competition between members of the senior management team. We've known of a number of cases in which the CEO accommodated the wishes of one or two members of senior management and made them voting directors. Sure enough, all the senior management team were clamoring for the same treatment. It's a principle of human nature that starts in the nursery and follows us into respectable, powerful adulthood: "He has one, so why can't I?" And some entrepreneurs have found the best defense is another saying familiar to us all: "If I give it to you, I have to give it to everyone."

Does that mean that management is effectively out of the loop of board discussions? Not at all. Members of the management team can be asked to make formal presentations to the board or even to sit in on board meetings without having a vote. In fact, some entrepreneurs who have decided to keep inside directors to a minimum find it useful to have senior management team members in on board meetings on a rotating basis. Because these managers are involved with day-to-day operations, their input is important. They can also provide informed feedback on the ramifications of various proposals. A similar nonvoting role can be carved out for the company legal counsel. For obvious reasons, it can be quite helpful to have objective legal counsel present at board meetings.

Although the entrepreneur may not feel he needs *more* than one other insider on the board as a voting member, he should have at least one. The entrepreneur will want someone with an insider perspective with whom to talk things over and exchange views after board meetings. An inside director can also test board ideas internally in day-to-day operations of the company.

Given that the number of seats on a board are limited, the issue of who should fill those seats is of paramount importance. The board should be made up of people with a wide diversity of experience, talents, and backgrounds. Typically, the entrepreneur will want someone with a financial background, someone with legal experience, someone with industry-specific and/or marketing background, and—depending on the type of company—someone with a technological background. The entrepreneur will want someone who has "been there before." Someone who has already had success in meeting the same challenges the entrepreneur now faces. Board members should be people with good business experience and a wide range of business contacts. Candidates can come from business or academia; they can be lawyers; they can be retirees or executives from non-competing companies.

Personality plays a big role when choosing a board. The board must be able to work well with the management team and, in particular, with the CEO or entrepreneur. We had one client, Bob Jones, of a defense contracting firm, who was a very brusque and domineering individual. One of his board members was a retired admiral from the navy, a brilliant but touchy man of tremendous pride. The admiral was used to a certain amount of deference, even from civilians. Bob Jones had never been deferential to anyone in his life. Although the admiral brought valuable insights and contacts to the company, he and the CEO rubbed each other the wrong way. Even when they agreed on something, they would somehow get into arguments. The board was spending so much of its time smoothing ruffled feathers that very little else was getting accomplished. Eventually, the admiral stepped down; the personality conflict had proved unsolvable.

Board members have a legal responsibility to monitor the actions of the CEO and the management team. However, within that obligation, there is also room for loyalty. The entrepreneur needs people who will tell him what they honestly think, but who are on his side—people who see their role as helping him run his company in the service of his vision. Being confident of the loyalty of board members means the entrepreneur can really listen to what the board member has to say, without worrying about the board member's motives.

The final question in forming a board is compensation. Outside directors are either paid an annual retainer fee or an attendance fee. Oftentimes, there is also a committee chair's fee. Retainer fees can range from a few thousand dollars to more than $50,000 at large corporations; attendance fees go from a few hundred dollars per meeting to more than $1,000. However, as companies have come under greater pressure to link the interests of their outside directors with the interests of their shareholders, it's become increasingly popular to use company stock, stock options, or phantom stock as a means of compensation. This is particularly true for publicly held companies. Paying directors with stock directly links their compensation to the performance of the company.

## THE OPERATIONS OF A BOARD

The function of a board of directors is to meet. Therefore, meetings—how they're scheduled and how they're run—are crucial to a board's success. Most meet quarterly, with the understanding that special circumstances (e.g. a pending significant acquisition, the resignation of a senior member of management, etc.) may require a special meeting. In addition, committees of the board may be established to deal with particular subjects. Board members are usually busy people; meetings should be scheduled well in advance so they can set aside time to attend. Many companies schedule meetings a year in advance around the key dates of the business year—for instance, when the company does its sales forecasts, its budget, the year-end review, and the midyear budget review.

There should be an agenda for every board meeting, and the chair should make sure that the discussion stays on point. It's all too easy for a group discussion about an important point to get diverted into a debate about minor details. The board doesn't meet often and its time is valuable; if they spend half an hour talking about an interesting but irrelevant side issue, that's half an hour they can't spend talking about something that could be critical to the company's future. If significant issues arise, a special meeting should be considered. When issues arise regularly—such as the annual audit or management compensation—subcommittees can be formed to deal with the matters and then recommend their conclusions to the board as a whole. This can save time as well as provide better focus.

If an agenda is too crowded, it will prevent meaningful discussion about any of the items, and it is this discussion that can be an invaluable tool for the entrepreneur, if he is listening carefully. Present in that room will be people with a huge store of expertise and experience, gathered together to help the entrepreneur attain his goals.

If most of what a board does is meet, most of what a board needs in order to be effective and productive is information. Directors must be kept up-to-date with the latest financial information, strategic business plans, financing arrangements, expansion plans, etc.

That doesn't mean the directors need to know every detail of the day-to-day functions of the company. That's the job of management. It is because the directors are *above* the day-to-day fray that they may have the distance to give good objective advice.

It also doesn't mean the directors should be inundated with paper. The board members need enough information to be able to understand issues, give advice, and make decisions—but no more. Executive summaries are usually sufficient, with more information provided on request.

And it certainly doesn't mean that directors should be inundated with paper at the meeting itself. Information should be provided in advance, and board members have a responsibility to arrive at the meeting having already read the material. Meetings are for discussing information, not learning it.

What information should be held back from the board? Nothing. Nobody likes to give bad news, but the board must be told everything. When sales are down, profits are disappointing, or an important deal is about to fall through—these are precisely the times when an entrepreneur needs the advice and guidance of experienced professionals who've been there before.

Besides written presentations, board members may want to speak directly to company employees. The board should be provided access to whoever they want to talk to, but CEOs generally need to keep an eye on employee-board communications. You don't want different employees giving different versions of the same information to the board, because it will create confusion.

## THE BOARD'S AGENDA

How boards actually work varies widely from company to company. Some CEOs use their boards as extensions of their management teams, discussing everything of importance with them; other CEOs want their boards to confine themselves to an oversight role. Regardless of how the CEO uses his board, the agenda for a board meeting should include the following:

- Review financial performance

- Review general business and industry trends and their impact on the company

- Provide input and critique management business plans and projections

- Approve key decisions such as payment of dividends, election of officers, significant financial transactions, new financing arrangements, leases, capital expenditures, information technology initiatives, mergers and acquisitions, etc.

- Review legal matters concerning the company

- Evaluate the performance of senior management, including the CEO

Although we've separated out the functions of a board, clearly many of these tasks are interrelated. Reviewing the company's financial performance and trends in business and its industry and their projected impact on the company inevitably leads to an evaluation of the company's business plans and projections.

This, in fact, is one of the board's most valuable functions—being available to discuss the big picture with the CEO. In the day-to-day storm of detail and decision making that goes into running a company, neither the CEO nor his management team may have much time to think about the future. A board meeting provides a time and place for the CEO to step back and talk about where the company is going.

Boards can also be extremely useful in helping CEOs to solve problems. A good example of this is the case of Fantel Fashions, an apparel company headquartered in New York. The son of the CEO had opened a factory to manufacture clothes in Florida. During the first two years, the margins were perilously thin. By the third year, it was losing money. The CFO would have liked to have raised the possibility of rethinking the viability of the factory, but how do you tell your boss to fire his son?

The situation worried the board as well. Finally, after watching the factory lose money for the second year in a row, one of the board members, a retired executive in the garment industry with over 30 years of experience, spoke up. "Look at the numbers," he said. "If you were buying overseas, your margins would be much better. The cost of the factory is simply too high in Florida. You have to face it. I know you wanted to give your son an opportunity, but things can't go on this way. It's time to face facts. We have to close the factory."

So the CEO did. It was something no one else could have said to him.

The board member got the company in touch with some vendor representatives in Hong Kong who were able to find suppliers who could produce the same goods for two thirds of what it had cost to make them in Florida. He also suggested that Fantel use a public warehouse rather than continue to run its own in New Jersey. With production and distribution outsourced, Fantel's profitability began to rise.

Using the board of directors to help make the tough decisions can free up the entrepreneur to do what he does best, and keep personalities out of the decision-making process.

Some of those tough decisions involve compensation and benefits, appointing new members to the board, and safeguarding the company's assets. Typically, the board of directors set up committees to handle these issues.

- The *compensation committee* is usually responsible for approving all company compensation and benefit programs. These include salaries, bonuses, stock options, pensions, and savings plans. The compensation committee has to approve the pay of the CEO and other top executives in senior management. Sometimes it is also responsible for reviewing organizational changes in the company. And it frequently plays a major role when senior management succession is an issue.

- The *nominating committee* nominates candidates for the board. The CEO has to work closely with this committee because the nominees have to be people with whom he feels comfortable. Some CEOs don't bother with a separate nominating committee; they use the entire board as their nominating committee. The advantage of having a committee is that the committee can hold get-to-know-you meetings with candidates and save the board time by doing preliminary screening.

- The *audit committee* is a very important committee for all boards. Publicly held companies are required to have an audit committee, generally at least two of whose members are outside or independent directors. The audit committee is charged with ensuring that the company's assets are being safeguarded. They must make sure that there is a strong system of internal controls in place and that the accounting and financial reporting practices are sound and appropriate.

  The audit committee liases with the internal audit staff of the company and with the outside auditors. Usually, they will meet with auditors before an audit to review the scope of the audit and address their areas of concern with the auditors. They also meet with the auditors after the audit is over to discuss significant issues identified during the audit, as well as the auditors' recommendations for improvements to the accounting and financial-reporting practices of the company.

Another important function of the audit committee is to provide a forum for sensitive accounting issues at a company. If employees or auditors suspect wrongdoing is being committed by management or being ignored by management, they can go to the audit committee. In our experience, because the audit committee is made up principally of outside directors, these issues will be treated with a high level of sensitivity and urgency, and will be addressed immediately.

The board can also establish an executive committee with the power to act on its behalf between board meetings, and a finance committee for reviewing financial questions. However, the current trend is to deemphasize or eliminate these committees entirely because they detract from the efficacy of the full board. Many companies just use the executive committee for emergencies and the financial committee, if they have one at all, to review unusual matters such as financial restructuring or new stock offerings.

There can also be specialized committees such as public affairs, social responsibility, environmental affairs, or employee benefits. However, most companies, in an effort to keep their board structure simple and flexible, will usually limit themselves to a nominating committee, an audit committee, and a compensation committee.

## WHY NOT A BOARD?

A board of directors rounds out the management team; it provides the entrepreneur with sage advice, a sounding board for new ideas, valuable contacts and introductions, someone to blame for unpleasant decisions, support for his plans for succession—but most important, it is an apparatus to provoke thoughtful discussion *within* the company. In preparing for board meetings, the management team is forced to examine its decisions from a fresh perspective. In putting together timely reports and numbers, the team is forced to be rigorous in its self-assessment. By having to persuade a group of intelligent outsiders of the soundness of its plans, a team must think through all the issues in advance. And by having to explain its purpose to the board, the management team will sometimes rediscover that purpose itself.

## ENTREPRENEUR'S SUMMARY

A board of directors fills an important infrastructural role for an entrepreneurial company. It rounds out the management team by offering valuable input and advice, acting as a sounding board, providing business contacts and introductions as a company moves into new arenas, taking the responsibility and the blame when tough decisions need to be made, sending a message to the outside world that the company is fiscally and morally responsible, and—as we have already stated in chapter seven—by aiding in succession planning.

In forming a board there are various issues that the entrepreneur needs to consider, including the make-up of the board, its function, and its agenda.

1. A board should be made up of between 5 and 12 members, have a higher percentage of outside members (independent nonemployees) than inside members (employees/officers of the company) and be able to work well with the management team and, in particular, with the CEO or entrepreneur. Outside directors are usually paid an annual retainer fee, but increasingly they are being paid with stock options to more closely bind their interests with those of the stockholders or owners of the company.

2. The function of a board of directors is to meet. To enhance the quality of these meetings, a company must pay attention to scheduling and proper preparation. This means the early and accurate dissemination of information.

3. The typical agenda for a board of directors meeting would include reviewing of financial performance; reviewing general business and industry trends and their impact on the company; providing input and critiquing management business plans and projections; approving key decisions such as

payment of dividends, election of officers, significant financial transactions; reviewing legal matters concerning the company; and evaluating the performance of senior management, including the CEO.

To maximize the effectiveness of the board, several committees are commonly formed. These include the compensation committee (responsible for approving company compensation and benefit programs), the nominating committee (which nominates candidates for the board), and the audit committee (which ensures that the company's assets are being safeguarded).

# Appendix A: Establishing Effective Employment Practices

# ESTABLISHING EFFECTIVE EMPLOYMENT PRACTICES

By
Peter M. Panken, Esq.
Parker Chapin Flattau & Klimpl, LLP
1211 Avenue of the Americas
New York, New York 10036
(212) 704-6000

All employees have a contract with their employers. If the terms are not spelled out in writing their disputes can lead to costly litigation. The following Manual can serve as a check list of how to establish typical terms. You will have to modify it to fit your operation, preferably in consultation with an employment lawyer. Areas where special thought will be needed are put in brackets "[ ]."

## I. HIRING

Laws and regulations of federal, state and local governments contain voluminous detail on legal procedures employers must observe to ensure that their hiring practices are not discriminatory or otherwise unlawful.

Everyone making a hiring decision today must realize that it might wind up being second-guessed by a judge or jury in an antidiscrimination suit.

Obviously, therefore, those involved in the screening and hiring process at a Company should be aware of the relevant laws and how to make sure that rejected applicants are not given grounds for lawsuits.

At the federal level such laws protect job applicants and, in some cases, employees from discrimination based on age (if they are over 40), color, national origin, pregnancy, race, religion, disability and gender. Members of these groups are given special protections.

Additional requirements are found in many states and cities. Illinois law makes it illegal to use an unfavorable discharge from military service as a reason for not hiring an individual. The District of Columbia bars discrimination "for any reason but merit" including, but not limited, "race, color, national origin, sex, age, marital status, personal appearance, sexual orientation, family responsibilities, political affiliation, disability, source of income, and place of residence or business."

In the federal courts, an unsuccessful job applicant seeking redress must assume the responsibility of proving the rejection was based either on illegal

-1-

discrimination or on grounds that, while apparently legal, still tended to eliminate members of a protected class to a disproportionate extent.

A rejected applicant belonging to a protected class must prove that he or she was qualified for the job but was rejected in favor of someone not a member of a protected class or that the job has gone unfilled.

In response to a complaint, an employer must offer justification for a hiring decision, which then gives the plaintiff an opening to argue that the reason was pretext for illegal discrimination.

Stakes can be high. In addition to legal expenses, an employer losing a suit could face a court order to hire the plaintiff, pay all accumulated back wages and between $50,000 and $300,000 for pain and suffering or punitive damages, or where willful discrimination because of age is proved -- pay double damages.

So an interviewer who made a hiring recommendation must be able to articulate the factors that shaped the decision. If the decision is challenged by a rejected applicant, the Company must offer persuasive justification for its choice.

And everything an interviewer has written, said, or is quoted as having said can be probed in a lawsuit for evidence that contradicts the proffered justification or reveals even a glimmer of illegal discriminatory intent.

How does an employer head off problems related to accusations of hiring discrimination?

Remember that being fair, well intentioned and making hiring decisions in an unbiased manner may not be enough to prevent costly lawsuits.

You might still wind up having to convince the judge or jury of your good intentions while being grilled by a relentless attorney who is being paid to make you look bad.

Here are some steps you can take to protect yourself:

1. Document your Company's compliance posture in detail. Issue to all interviewers memos stating that your Company hires only on the basis of relevant considerations. Remember that each piece of paper dealing with hiring is a potential trial exhibit that can buttress your case or, if you are not careful, work against you.

2. Avoid irrelevant questions during an interview. Any question asked will be assumed to reflect a selection criterion. Questions unrelated to business may be viewed as evidence of hidden illegal motivation. For

example, inquiring when the applicant graduated from school is usually irrelevant to job performance, but often reveals the applicant's age.

3. Do not offer applicants reasons of rejection unless, and until, you are forced to. Many cases are lost because a harried interviewer casually gives a rejected job-seeker a reason for rejection without taking time to think the implications through. You are choosing those you think are the cream of the applicants, so you can honestly say: "We selected those we thought would work out best."

4. Do not tell applicants they were, or were not, qualified for the job. State only that, in your opinion, the ones selected had better qualifications. Otherwise, such explanations -- everything you said or wrote -- can be used against you. Excluding applicants on the basis of a stated qualification leaves you vulnerable if a jury does not agree that there is a valid business reason for using that criterion.

5. Apply prerequisites consistently and even-handedly. Do not offer in-house training to young, nonminority or male "go-getters" while requiring others to undergo the same training before they are hired.

6. Make applicants specify in their applications exactly the type of job they are seeking, and then have them document their own qualifications for that job. That way, they select themselves out of the pool for other jobs, and you are not responsible for considering skills they have not revealed.

7. Beware of making casual, short-hand comments on applications or notes during an interview. Interviewer's notations like "nice girl" or "mature" on rejected applications have been used in court to support a judgment of sex or age discrimination.

8. Review job descriptions. Be sure they are free of irrelevant criteria that act to exclude members of protected classes.

9. Be consistent. Do not bend the rules for some and not for others -- especially where minorities and women are not the beneficiaries.

10. Actions speak louder than words. Analyze your hiring practices by race, sex and even age. If you are rejecting certain minorities, or women, at a higher rate than white males, you may be courting an expensive lawsuit. You may need expert legal advice, so you can make your hiring practice analysis effectively.

-3-

Finally, include in your application a statement as follows above the signature line:

I understand and agree as follows:

If I am employed: (i) I will follow all Company rules and will perform any duties which may be assigned to me at any time, (ii) my employment is for no fixed term and may be curtailed or terminated at any time in the Company's sole discretion for any reason not contrary to law, (iii) I will work whatever days, hours and overtime as the Company requires, and (iv) my hours and days of work are not guaranteed, and may be changed at any time and from time to time by the Company.

I completed this application truthfully and completely. If I have not fully and honestly completed this application, the firm may reject my application or dismiss me from employment at any time. I authorize the Company to verify all of my answers to this application and to disseminate the information I gave on this application to any person or entity.

I authorize all persons or entities listed in this application to give the firm any information regarding me and hereby release the Company, its agents, and all of said persons or entities from all liability to me.

None of the above provisions may be waived or modified by the Company unless in writing and signed by the _____ of the Company.

I have read and understand the above and agree to it.

## II. <u>SETTING THE RULES OF EMPLOYMENT</u>

Once hired, employers may be best protected if they put employees on notice of what they can expect from the Company as well as what is expected from them. An employment manual is one of the more effective means of communicating expectations.

-4-

## MODEL EMPLOYEE MANUAL

### WELCOME TO THE COMPANY

As an employee, you will be expected to carry out your job functions in a professional manner being ever mindful [insert discription of business] that our customers are of paramount importance.

This policy handbook summarizes some of the Company's employment practices and the benefits to which you are entitled as our employee [except where an applicable collective bargaining agreement provides for different terms and conditions of your employment.] Your benefits are more accurately described in our benefit manuals, which are consistently reviewed and modified as the need arises. If there are any differences between this handbook and Company procedure or benefit manuals, the procedure or benefit manual prevails.

The Company, in its sole discretion, reserves the right, at any time, to amend, modify, alter or terminate any statements or policies in this handbook as well as any employee benefits.

### YOUR SALARY

### WHEN YOU ARE PAID

The payroll week runs from Monday to Sunday of each week. You will be paid each subsequent Thursday following the completion of the work week. Your check will reflect your compensation for the prior work week less required payroll deductions. [It is important to check state labor laws for rules as to when and how (cash or check) wages must be paid.]

### DEDUCTIONS FROM YOUR PAYCHECK

Deductions will be made from your paycheck as required by law (including your federal and state withholding taxes, and your portion of Social Security contributions as well as any garnishments, or any other deductions required by law) or, where applicable, as you request for contributions to Company programs such as pension or health insurance.

Your deductions will be itemized on your payroll stub. You should review your paycheck stub carefully each payday. If, at any time, you have any questions about the amounts shown on your paycheck or how they are calculated, you should contact the [Payroll] Department.

-5-

Tax withholding is based on the number of dependents you claim on the W-4 form which you completed. Each employee is responsible for the accuracy of that form and for up-dating the information when necessary. W-4 forms are available in the Human Resources Department.

## OVERTIME

Overtime may be required when necessitated by business operations. If asked to work, you will be expected to cooperate. Certain employees will receive pay at the rate of 1½ times their regular rate for all hours worked in excess of 40 hours, in any work week, excluding meal periods, unless otherwise required by law. If you are entitled to overtime pay at 1½ times your regular rate, you will be notified by your supervisor. If you have any questions, ask your supervisor or the Personnel Department.

[Be especially careful about salaried employees who may not be exempt from overtime under federal Fair Labor Standards Act or State laws. In general, bona fide executives with weekly salaries of at least $250 who supervise at least two full time employees and whose "primary duty" is the management of a recognized subdivision of the organization are exempt. Secretaries, administrative assistants etc. are not exempt. Certain Administrators and Professionals also may be exempt. But these laws are tricky and not easily understood so you should talk to a professional about the exemptions before failing to pay time and one-half for hours worked over 40 in a work week.]

## EMPLOYEE BENEFIT PLANS

The Company provides the following Employee Benefit Plans for eligible employees:

- Group Health Insurance

- 401(k) Plan

- Pension Plan

- Accidental Death and Dismemberment Insurance

- Life Insurance

- Short-Term (1-26 weeks) and Long-Term (over 26 weeks) Disability Income Protection

-6-

The requirements for enrollment in each of these plans vary. New employees are not eligible for at least their first [ninety] days of employment. Eligible employees will be contacted at the appropriate time regarding enrollment for these benefits and a Summary Plan Description will be provided. The Company, in its sole discretion, reserves the right to amend, modify, alter or terminate any or all of these plans at any time. If you wish to review the benefit booklets for any of these plans, contact the Personnel Department in writing.

[Most of these plans are covered by the Employee Retirement Income Security Act which requires a separate summary plan description which your provider will usually prepare.]

## VACATIONS

### REGULAR FULL-TIME EMPLOYEES

All regular full-time employees who are actively employed are eligible for paid vacation based upon their anniversary dates of hire:

| Length of Continuous Employment | Vacation |
| --- | --- |
| after completing 1 year | 2 weeks |
| after completing 5 years | 3 weeks |
| after completing 10 years | 4 weeks |
| after completing 15 years | 5 weeks |

[If employee works variable hours it will be important to spell out how much vacation pay is - e.g. 40 hours pay, weekly base salary, 1/52 last year's W-2 wages, etc.]

### REGULAR PART-TIME EMPLOYEES

Regular part-time employees who work a minimum of 20 hours in a work week are eligible for one-half the paid vacation of a regular full-time employee, based on the same vacation schedule set forth above. As a regular part-time employee, your vacation pay will be calculated on the average weekly wages during the twelve (12) full weeks preceding your vacation.

### SCHEDULING VACATIONS

It is the responsibility of Managers to schedule vacation in cooperation with their employees to assure that each employee receives a full vacation and that there is adequate coverage of the work to be done.

-7-

As a matter of policy, vacations should be taken in increments of one (1) full week.

Employee vacation preferences will be granted subject to the staffing needs of the Company.

If a holiday or holidays occur during an employee's vacation, the holiday or holidays will not be considered as part of the vacation period. In such cases, the employee will receive an extra day or days as vacation and will be paid for the additional day or days where eligible.

## VACATION PAY

Employees eligible for vacation payment will receive their vacation pay on the day before the start of their vacation.

## VACATION ACCRUAL

All vacation must be taken in the year following the year in which it is earned. There is no carry over of unused vacation from one year to the next. If you do not use your vacation for the year, you will lose it.

## HOLIDAYS

## REGULAR FULL-TIME EMPLOYEES

Each regular full-time employee will be entitled to the scheduled holidays listed below:

New Year's Day
Martin Luther King's Birthday Celebration
President's Day
Memorial Day
Fourth of July
Labor Day
Thanksgiving Day
Veterans Day or Day after Thanksgiving
Christmas Day
Birthday - Floating Holiday
Personal Day - Floating Holiday

Floating holidays may be taken on any work day you and your manager agree upon, subject to the staffing needs of your department.

[The number and dates of holidays will vary depending on business needs and may vary from location to location.]

-8-

## REGULAR PART-TIME EMPLOYEES

Each regular part-time employee working a minimum of 20 hours each week with continuous active employment for twelve months will be entitled to the scheduled holidays listed below:

New Year's Day
Memorial Day
Fourth of July
Labor Day
Thanksgiving Day
Christmas Day

## PAY FOR HOLIDAYS

Employees eligible for holidays shall be paid for the hours they were regularly scheduled to work on the holiday if they work their full schedule on their first regularly scheduled work day immediately prior to the holiday, on the holiday if scheduled, and on the first regularly scheduled work day immediately following the holiday.

Due to the nature of our business, it is often necessary for employees to work holidays. Those employees who work a scheduled holiday will be paid [at the rate of time and one-half (or their regular rate)] for the hours they work on the holiday [in addition to their holiday pay] or will be given another day off with pay.

## EXCUSED ABSENCE BEFORE OR AFTER A HOLIDAY

An employee who is absent due to illness on the day before or after a holiday will only be eligible for holiday pay by presenting proof of illness satisfactory to the Company. An employee who is absent from work due to jury duty will be eligible for holiday pay by submitting certification of actual jury duty service.

## EMPLOYEES ON LEAVE

Employees who are on layoff or disability, family and medical leave or any other leave at the time the holiday occurs are not entitled to receive holiday pay.

-9-

## PERSONAL DAYS

Regular full-time employees who have completed one year of employment will be entitled to two paid personal days each year. Personal days may be used, at your discretion, for religious observance or any other purpose.

Employees must use their personal days in the year earned. You may not accumulate personal days. Instead, at the end of the calendar year, the Company will pay an employee for any unused personal days.

During the first year of employment you will be eligible to take one personal day off with pay after you have completed six months of employment.

## JURY DUTY

After six (6) months of continuous employment, if you are a regular full-time employee required to serve as a juror, the Company will pay you the difference between your jury duty pay and the regular straight time pay for any scheduled work time that you miss during the first two (2) weeks of your jury duty. To be reimbursed, you must present a court voucher and proof of actual jury duty service.

Employees serving on jury duty shall have Saturdays and Sundays as days off during the term of such service, regardless of their normally scheduled work shifts.

To receive jury duty pay, employees must provide the Company with a copy of the Jury Duty Notice as soon as it is received.

An employee required to be available for jury duty, but not required to be in court, must report to work. Utilization of the court call-in system, if available, is required in order to receive jury duty pay.

## BEREAVEMENT LEAVE

After a death in the immediate family of any employee, the Company provides up to three (3) consecutive days of bereavement leave without loss of pay beginning with the date of death and ending with and/or including the day after the funeral or final services.

For each bereavement leave day the employee was scheduled to work, an employee may receive pay in an amount equivalent to the number of hours the employee was scheduled to work that day. An employee may be required to submit proof of death and/or funeral date.

-10-

Immediate family includes current spouse, parent, step-parents, parent-in-law, step parent-in-law, grandparent, child, step-child, grandchild, sibling and step-sibling.

If a death in the family occurs, you should notify your Supervisor or Manager as to the anticipated length of your absence.

## ILLNESS

Regular full-time employees will be eligible for up to five (5) paid sick leave days during each calendar year after completion of a year of continuous employment.

Regular full-time employees in their first employment year will be eligible for paid sick leave days on a prorated basis as of the first month following ninety (90) calendar days of continuous active employment. The number of paid sick leave days for full time employees in their first employment year will be earned at the rate of one-half (½) day per month worked after completing ninety (90) days of continuous service.

The Company will not pay for unused sick leave days. However, unused sick leave days may be carried over into succeeding calendar years up to a maximum of 15 days.

If you should feel ill at work, tell your Supervisor or Manager. If your illness simply requires rest, you will be given an opportunity to do so. If your illness is more serious, arrangements will be made for you to go home, to the Company Medical Department or to a hospital. If it is decided that you should leave work, you will be paid for any time you have worked that day.

Employees missing work due to illness must call their Supervisor or Manager relating the type of sickness and expected return date. Failure to call your supervisor and manager each day you are out sick will result in disciplinary action.

If an employee misses five consecutive work days due to illness, the Company Medical Department must review the medical documentation and authorize your return to work.

The Company may, at any time, request that you provide a doctor's note or request that you be examined by the Company Medical Department.

[In New York and New Jersey, employees out for more than a week are entitled to disability insurance. Contact the [Human Resources] Department for claim forms.]

## FAMILY AND MEDICAL LEAVE

[Required for employers of 50 or more employees]

### Leave

In accordance with the Family and Medical Leave Act of 1993, the Company has established a policy that will allow up to 12 weeks of unpaid leave in a 12-month period commencing from the date of hire or the date the employee returned from the employee's 12-week Family and Medical Leave Act leave:

> for an employee's own serious health condition that makes the employee unable to perform the functions of the employee's job;

> for a serious health condition of an employee's child, spouse or parent where the employee is needed to care for that family member;

> upon the birth of a child to care for the child; or

> because of the placement of a child with an employee for adoption or foster care.

### Eligibility

In order to be eligible for Family and Medical Leave an employee must have worked for the Company:

> for at least 12 months; and

> for at least 1,250 hours during the year preceding the start of the leave.

### Return to Work

Unless otherwise permitted by law, at the end of the approved Family and Medical Leave, the employee will be offered restoration to the same position he/she held when leave commenced or to an equivalent position. The Company may choose to exempt certain highly compensated employees from this requirement and not return them to the same or an equivalent position.

An employee whose Family and Medical Leave exceeds 12 weeks within a 12-month period will not be guaranteed a job upon return from the leave, unless otherwise required by law.

-12-

[In some states, employers must provide for more than 12 weeks of leave. In Connecticut, for example, employers must provide up to 16 weeks of leave in a two-year period (for employers with 75+ employees). Therefore, employees would be permitted to take 16 weeks in the first year under state law and 12 weeks in the second year under the Family and Medical Leave Act].

An employee who fails to return to work at the end of an approved medical leave will be considered as having voluntarily terminated.

The Company requires that upon returning from leave due to an employee's serious health condition, the employee must provide Certification from his/her health care provider that the employee is able to resume work and that the employee is fit for duty with regard to the serious health condition that caused the employee's need for Family and Medical Leave.

Request for Leave

Employees must provide 30 days prior notice if the leave is foreseeable. If an employee is unable to provide such notice, notice must be provided as is practicable.

An employee undergoing planned medical treatment will be required to make a reasonable effort to schedule the treatment to minimize disruptions to the Company's operation.

Family and Medical Leave Request forms are available from the Human Resource Department. Requests for Family and Medical Leave should be made by completing a form and returning it to the Human Resource Department.

Certification

An employee requesting a Family and Medical Leave for a serious health condition must provide the Company with Certification from a health care provider.

The Human Resource Department has Certification forms for the health provider to complete. The forms must be fully completed.

The employee should furnish the required Certification when requesting leave or soon after the leave is requested, but not more than 15 calendar days from the start of the requested leave, unless it is not practical under the particular circumstances. During the leave, the Company may also require that the employee obtain recertification of the medical condition supporting the leave.

-13-

The Company has the right to require an employee to obtain an opinion by a health care provider designated and paid for by the Company either before or during the leave. If there is a disagreement, a third health care provider will settle the dispute.

### Disability/Workers Compensation Benefits

Employees on a Family and Medical Leave due to their own serious health condition may be eligible for payments from other sources such as Workers' Compensation, State Disability or disability insurance, if any. Employees should ask the [Human Resources Department] if they think they are eligible for these benefits.

### Intermittent Leave

If an employee requests intermittent leave it may be necessary for the Company to transfer him/her to another position that will better accommodate an intermittent or reduced schedule.

### Substitution of Paid Leave

Employees taking Family and Medical Leave to care for a child, spouse or parent with a serious health condition or for their own serious health condition must use all of their available accrued and unused paid sick and personal days and vacation as part of the leave.

Employees on Family and Medical Leave for the birth or the placement of a child must use all of their available accrued and unused vacation and personal days as part of the leave.

### Benefit Continuation

The Company will continue to maintain group health insurance coverage for the employee and, where applicable, for his-her dependents during the Family and Medical Leave, up to a maximum of 12 weeks in a 12-month period. Employees must, however, arrange to pay the premium contributions they previously had deducted in order to continue group health or other insurance for themselves and, where applicable, their dependents during the Family and Medical Leave. [Detail Company policy as to other benefits.]

If an employee fails to return to work at the end of the Family and Medical Leave, the Company may require the employee to reimburse it for the amount the Company paid for the employee's health insurance premiums during the leave.

### MILITARY LEAVE

-14-

Employees who are members of the Reserves or the National Guard will be granted, upon request, an unpaid leave of absence for military training duty. However, they must present their orders in advance to their Department Manager. Employees eligible for vacation may use their vacation for their military leave.

A military leave will also be granted to employees who enter active military service in the Armed Forces or who are ordered for an initial period of active duty for training in the Reserves or the National Guard. Employees will be paid for any unused vacation, if eligible, on a pro rata basis for that year in accordance with the terms of the vacation policy set forth in this Personnel Manual. Employees who return to work after an extended absence for military service are eligible for reinstatement in accordance with applicable law. They must, however, seek reinstatement within the required time limits and be qualified for work.

If you have any questions regarding military leave, please contact the Personnel Office.

### PERSONAL LEAVE

The Company is aware that an employee may need some time off from work to attend to personal situations which do not qualify as a Family and Medical Leave or any other leave provided by the Company.

Full-time employees may apply to their Supervisor or Manager, in writing, for an unpaid personal leave of absence not to exceed fourteen (14) consecutive days. The Personal Leave may be extended, in the Company's sole discretion and on such terms as the Company may impose, taking into consideration the need for an extension and staffing needs. Employees granted a leave extension will be returned to work at the end of the extension period if their position is open at that time.

Employees who are granted an unpaid personal leave of absence of up to fourteen (14) consecutive days continue to accrue credit for vacation.

If an employee fails to return to work at the end of the leave or is employed by or working for another employer or Company during the leave, employment with the Company will be considered voluntarily terminated.

## JOB PERFORMANCE REVIEWS

[Should be done at least annually and should always include a discussion of weaknesses and a plan to improve performance in the next year.]

All employees are expected to work efficiently and harmoniously and to meet the requirements and standards of their position.

During your employment with the Company, your Manager or his or her designee will evaluate your work. He or she will undertake a formal review of your work performance giving consideration at each review to changes in your job content or responsibility.

Your salary is monitored in this manner so that it accurately reflects your job and your performance. Based upon the evaluation of your Manager or his or her designee and your total work record, your salary may be increased. It should be understood, however, that increases in your salary are not an automatic part of the performance review but are within the Company's sole discretion based upon your entire work record and the evaluation of your Manager or his or her designee as well as the financial condition of the company.

## EQUAL EMPLOYMENT OPPORTUNITY

Our policy is to select, place, train and promote the best qualified individuals based upon relevant factors such as work quality, attitude and experience, so as to provide equal employment opportunity for all our employees in compliance with applicable local, state and federal laws and without regard to non-work-related factors such as race, color, religion/creed, sex, national origin, age, disability (where the employee or applicant has the ability to perform the essential functions of the job with or without reasonable accommodation), citizenship, marital status or sexual orientation.

This equal opportunity policy applies to all Company activities, including but not limited to, recruiting, hiring, training, transfers, promotions and benefits.

A fundamental policy of the Company is that the workplace is for work. Our goal is to provide a workplace free from tensions involving matters which do not relate to the Company's business. In particular, an atmosphere of tension created by nonwork-related conduct, including ethnic, racial, sexual or religious remarks, animosity, unwelcome sexual advances or requests for sexual favors or other such conduct does not belong in our workplace.

Sexual, racial or ethnic harassment of employees or of applicants by other employees is prohibited. Harassment includes, without limitation, verbal harassment (epithets, derogatory statements, slurs), physical harassment (assault,

-16-

physical interference with normal work or involvement), visual harassment (posters, cartoons, drawings), and innuendo.

Sexual harassment is a violation of state and federal law. It includes unwelcome sexual advances, requests for sexual favors, sexually motivated physical contact and other verbal or physical conduct, or visual forms of harassment of a sexual nature when submission to such conduct is either explicitly or implicitly made a term or condition of employment or is used as the basis for employment decisions or when such conduct has the purpose or effect of unreasonably interfering with an individual's work performance or creating an intimidating, hostile or offensive work environment.

You cannot be forced to submit to such conduct as a basis for any employment decision and the Company will do its best to keep itself free of any conduct which creates an intimidating, hostile or offensive work environment for our employees.

### WHAT TO DO IF YOU FEEL OUR POLICY HAS BEEN VIOLATED

In the event that any sort of ethnic, racial, religious, or sexual harassment, or similarly abusive verbal or physical conduct interferes with any individual's work performance or creates an intimidating, hostile or offensive work environment, we urge you to contact your Manager or Supervisor.

If you feel uncomfortable bringing the matter to your Manager or Supervisor or if your Manager or Supervisor is thought to be involved in the harassment, you may contact the Corporate [Personnel Manager or Vice President], who, to the extent possible, will treat the matter with the degree of confidentiality that you require. Charges of harassment will be promptly and thoroughly investigated and a report will be made to you concerning the results of the investigation.

If the Company determines that harassment has occurred, appropriate relief for the employee bringing the complaint and appropriate disciplinary action against the harasser, up to and including discharge, will follow. A non-employee who subjects an employee to harassment in the workplace will be informed of our Company's policy and appropriate action will be taken. In all cases, the Company will make follow-up inquiries to ensure that the harassment has not resumed.

An employee who remains unsatisfied after investigation by his/her Manager or Supervisor may seek review from the Corporate [Personnel Manager]. The Corporate [Personnel Manager] may direct or conduct an independent investigation, including witness interviews and statements concerning the complaint. Additionally, the Corporate Personnel Manager may take further remedial or disciplinary action as is appropriate.

The Company understands that these matters can be extremely sensitive, and so far as possible, will keep all employee complaints and all communications, such as interviews and witness statements in strict confidence.

The Company will not tolerate retaliation against any employee who complains of sexual harassment or provides information in connection with any such complaint.

## EMPLOYEE OBLIGATIONS

### YOUR RESPONSIBILITIES

Our Company has always maintained the highest standards of service. Therefore, in all dealings with the public and with each other, all Company employees are expected to respect the dignity of each individual. With the foregoing in mind, the Company has developed policies and rules for the benefit of us all.

Some of the policies have already been outlined earlier in the handbook. Others are contained in the following list. You are encouraged to read this list of actions and to understand them fully. Many of these things have never been a problem for the Company, and we hope to keep it that way. If any one of these actions or any one of the previously mentioned actions or similarly egregious action is taken by you, it can result in disciplinary action up to and including dismissal.

1. Improperly treating or servicing a fellow employee, customer or any other non-employee.

2. Insubordination or lack of cooperation.

3. Failing to follow Company job instructions.

4. Failing to follow instruction of, or to perform work requested by, a Supervisor or Manager.

5. Failing to meet a Company measure of efficiency and productivity.

6. Placing long distance personal phone calls or making or receiving excessive personal phone calls on Company time.

7. Unauthorized or excessive absences (including late arrival and early departure from work).

8. Sleeping on Company property or during the time in which you are supposed to be working.

9. Abusing, wasting or stealing Company property or the property of any Company employee or non-employee.

10. Removing Company property or records without written authorization.

11. Falsifying your employment application or other personnel records.

12. Falsifying Company reports or records (including timesheets).

13. Violating the law on Company premises, including gambling.

14. Fighting or starting a disturbance on Company premises or while performing job duties, including, but not limited to, assaulting or intimidating a Company employee or non-employee.

15. Unauthorized possession of firearms, weapons or dangerous substances while performing job duties or on Company premises.

16. Reporting to work in a condition unfit to perform your duties, including reporting to work with measurable amounts of illegal drugs or controlled substances in your system or being under the influence of alcohol or drugs or controlled substances.

17. Consuming or selling alcohol, illegal drugs or controlled substances on Company premises or while performing your job duties.

18. Smoking, eating and drinking in prohibited areas.

19. Violating a Company safety rule or practice or creating or contributing to unhealthful or unsanitary conditions.

20. Acting in conflict with the interests of the Company.

21. Disclosing confidential Company information without authorization.

-19-

22.    Unauthorized solicitation or distribution on Company property.

23.    Using profanity toward others.

24.    Failing to fully cooperate in any Company investigation.

All employees are expected to work efficiently and harmoniously and to meet the requirements and standards for their position.

## ATTENDANCE

The Company relies on you to report to work regularly and on time. If you are going to be late or absent, you must contact your Supervisor or Manager immediately. If you have to leave early, you must obtain approval from your Supervisor or Manager. Your Supervisor or Manager may require that you make up any lost work time.

The Company will take disciplinary action, up to and including discharge, where attendance is unacceptable.

## TELEPHONE USAGE

Contact with the public is vital to our business. Telephone courtesy is a priority because, to the public, yours may be the only Company voice on the phone.

- Answer the telephone promptly and identify yourself per departmental guidelines

- Make sure your telephone is attended when you are away

- Speak clearly

- Take careful and complete messages for co-workers

- Do not leave someone on hold for more than a few seconds

The Company recognizes that there may be an occasion when it is necessary to make or receive a personal call at work. Abuse of this privilege is subject to disciplinary action.

## CONFIDENTIALITY

-20-

As an employee of the Company you may learn confidential business information. During and after employment with the Company, confidential business information may not be shared with non-employees of the Company and may only be shared with Company employees on a need-to-know basis. If you violate this policy, disciplinary action will be taken up to and including immediate discharge.

The Company will provide employee information to outside agencies only upon written authorization of the employee or as provided by law. The Personnel and Payroll Departments are the only authorized departments for disclosure of information. Most banks, credit agencies, or other parties requiring employment information will provide you with an appropriate form. Authorization forms may also be obtained from the Personnel Department.

Our standard credit or other reference letters are limited to confirming dates of employment, job title, and current rate of pay. All requests for employment verification must be received by the Personnel Department in writing. Our response will be in writing unless special arrangements are made in advance with the Personnel Department. The Company does not provide letters of recommendation.

The Company protects employee's confidentiality and expects the employees to protect the Company's confidences as well. Supervisors may not give out any information about an employee and must refer any phone calls seeking such information to the Personnel Manager. Under no circumstances may a Supervisor or Manager verify employment over the phone.

In addition, the Company also expects that you respect the privacy of your fellow employees, both with employees and non-employees. Personal information about any employee may not be discussed with other employees or non-employees without written Company authorization.

## DRUG AND ALCOHOL POLICY

To help insure a safe, healthy, and productive work environment for our employees and others, to protect Company property, and to insure efficient operations, the Company has adopted a policy of maintaining a workplace free of drugs and alcohol.

Individuals under the influence of drugs and alcohol on the job pose serious safety and health risks not only to themselves, but also to all those who surround or come in contact with the user. Therefore, possessing, using, consuming, purchasing, distributing, manufacturing, dispensing or selling alcohol or controlled substances, or having alcohol or controlled substances in your system without medical authorization during your work hours, on Company premises or

-21-

while on duty will result in disciplinary action up to and including immediate termination.

[Employers who are subject to the Federal Drug Free Workplace Act should also add the following: In accordance with the Federal Drug Free Workplace Act, employees must notify the Company of any criminal drug statute conviction for a violation occurring in the workplace no later than 5 days after such conviction. Failure to timely notify the Company of a conviction for a criminal drug statute violation occurring in the workplace will be subject to disciplinary action up to and including termination.]

## SOLICITATION AND DISTRIBUTION

Because distraction on the job leads to unsafe working conditions, poor work performance and inefficiency, we have established the following rules:

- During periods of your workday when you are engaged in or required to be performing your work tasks, you may not engage in solicitation of other employees or distribution of literature for any purpose.

- During periods in another employee's workday when he or she is engaged in or required to be performing his or her work tasks, you may not solicit the other employee for any purpose.

- Distribution of literature of any kind may not be made in the work areas of the premises at any time.

- Persons not employed by the Company are not permitted to solicit or distribute literature on Company premises.

## EMPLOYEE PRIVACY EXPECTATIONS

## INSPECTION

The Company reserves the right to search any person or article entering on its property or off-site while performing services for the Company and to search property, equipment and storage areas including but not limited to, clothing, personal effects, vehicles, buildings, rooms, facilities, offices, parking lots, desks, cabinets, lunch and equipment boxes or bags and equipment. Any items which you do not want to have inspected should not be brought to work.

## EMPLOYEE INFORMATION

## PERSONNEL RECORDS

-22-

Each employee is responsible for updating personnel information with the Personnel Department in writing when there is a change in address, telephone number, marital status, emergency contact, or number and names of dependents.

Tax information must be kept current. W-4 forms are available in the Personnel Department throughout the year.

All records maintained by the Personnel Department are the property of the Company. Employees may view their Personnel files in the presence of the Human Resource Manager or a designee. No material may be removed from the file or duplicated by an employee but an employee may insert comments if desired.

Personnel material is shared within the Company only on a need-to-know basis.

## TERM OF EMPLOYMENT

[In New Jersey this should be put at the front of the Manual.]

Unless you are given a written contract signed by the President specifying an employment term, your employment is "at will." This means that both the Company and the employee have the right to terminate employment at any time with or without cause. Nothing in this handbook nor any oral or written representation by any employee, official, Manager, or Supervisor of this Company shall be construed as a contract of employment, unless the President signs a written contract of employment.

## MISCELLANEOUS PROVISIONS

## POLICIES SUBJECT TO CHANGE

The Company continually reviews its personnel policies and employee benefits and reserves the right, in its sole discretion, to modify, supplement, amend or delete any of the provisions contained in this Handbook or any employee benefits at any time. This Handbook does not represent the entire policies of the Company but is designed to give guidance to many essential Company personnel policies.

## ACKNOWLEDGMENT

[Always get a signed receipt]

I hereby acknowledge that I received my Handbook describing Company policies and my benefits as an employee of the Company. I have read and

-23-

understand the Company policies contained herein and am fully aware of my obligations at all times to fully comply with the responsibilities that are imposed on me as a condition of employment.

DATE_____          SIGNATURE_____

NAME (Please Print)_____

## II. Termination Without Tears

At the other end of the employment spectrum is termination. Here again the litigation risk can be high.

At one time, firings were financially painful only for employees. Increasingly, however, terminated employees are suing and collecting from former employers. Whether an employee can recover depends on who was fired and why, and on which law applies and on what the jury decides.

### The Protected Classes

Federal and many state laws prohibit termination based on, for example, race, sex, national origin, color, disability, union activity, age and even protesting discrimination. Aggrieved employees can file charges with state human rights agencies and the federal Equal Employment Opportunity Commission, the federal National Labor Relations Board and the Department of Labor. If these agencies don't help, lawyers will gladly sue.

In many states, employees have won suits on allegations that they were fired for filing workers' compensation claims, serving on juries or refusing to participate in practices they considered unprofessional, unethical or illegal.

In most states if the terminated employee contends that a personnel manual or somebody in authority said that employment would be "permanent" or that termination would be only for "just cause," the employee is entitled to a trial to determine whether the reason for termination was sufficient. In a few states, like Massachusetts and New Hampshire, even if nothing is said in the manual there is an implied obligation to act in good faith in terminating employees.

Employees who win such suits can win big -- reinstatement, back pay, future lost pay, damages for pain and suffering, and if a jury thinks the employer acted

-24-

wilfully or maliciously, even punitive damages. Multi-million dollar verdicts are possible.

All this means that every termination must be treated as if it could be attacked in court. Once in court, the employer must present a reason for the termination that is not inconsistent with any statute or other law. During that litigation all the Company's records on this employee and others in similar situations can be brought into court and will have to be explained to a judge or jury whose decision will turn on some notion of fairness and justice.

## What Happens in Termination Litigation

Terminated plaintiffs most commonly claim they were terminated "because" they were members of a group protected from employment discrimination by federal and state laws. To prevail, the terminee must prove that protected group status was the determining factor in their selection for adverse treatment.

This issue normally turns on the intent of the employer. The only direct evidence of intent is the testimony of the actor, but triers of fact are skeptical of testimony of sanctimonious intent.

The courts have, therefore, developed a complicated scheme of presumptions and shifting burdens to give plaintiffs a fair chance to reach the trier of fact without encouraging frivolous lawsuits.

1. The Employee's "Prima Facie" Case Burden

The employee may force the employer to articulate its reasons for selecting the plaintiff by establishing a prima facie case (sometimes called raising a presumption of illegal discriminatory intent) by showing:

membership in a protected class (race, sex, age, etc.),

termination (or some other adverse employment action), and

that someone not in the protected class received better treatment.

2. The Employer's Burden to Articulate a Legal Reason

The burden of production (but not persuasion) then shifts to the employer to articulate a non-discriminatory business reason for its actions.

3. The Presumption of Illegality Disappears

-25-

The prima facie presumption then disappears from the case and plaintiffs still have the burden of proving they were terminated because they were protected class members.

Plaintiff has the burden and opportunity to get to the trier of fact by showing that "a discriminatory reason more likely motivated the employer" or "that the employer's proffered explanation is unworthy of credence." Plaintiff may do this in a variety of ways including:

- Showing there is a statistically significant adverse impact on members of the protected classes which is not explainable by business reasons. (Actions speak louder than words.)

- Actual admissions of illegal intent by authorized agents of the employer who participated in or influenced the action. (Anything an employer or agent says can be used against them.)

- Anecdotal testimony usually about statements made by supervisors tending to show illegal intent (in effect, smoking gun statements). ("A smile and a suitcase," 'the old fellow's lost it," "that ethnic group is just lazy," etc.)

- Evidence tending to show that the articulated reason is untrue. Because employers are presumably reasonable, the only reason to lie is to cover up illegal intent to discriminate (this begins to sound a lot like the notion of consciousness of guilt which arose in criminal cases), and/or

- Inconsistent statements made by someone who speaks for the employer (everyone had better be on the same wave length).

4. Defendants then Have an Opportunity (and Burden) to Show It Would Have Happened Anyway

Finally, if the plaintiff establishes "direct evidence" that discriminatory intent was "a determining factor" in their selection (whatever "direct evidence" may be), the employer is given an opportunity to prove that the plaintiff would have been treated in the same manner notwithstanding the proven fact that a discriminatory motive played a part in the decision. Such proof will limit judicial remedies to declaratory and/or injunctive relief and attorneys' fees and costs and save the employer from an award of damages and/or an order requiring admission, reinstatement, hiring or promotion of the plaintiff or payment of back pay.

**What Employers Stand To Lose**

Losing employment discrimination litigation means the employer pays two people for the same work: the retained employee and the terminee. Losing an age discrimination claim can mean paying three times because a terminated employee wins double damages if the plaintiff shows that the unlawful age discrimination was "willful." Losing a federal discrimination claim concerning sex, national origin or religion can add up to $50,000 to $300,000 damages for "pain and suffering," future "pecuniary losses" or even punitive damages if the judge or jury despises the employer. There is no cap for race discrimination. And many states allow recovery of punative damages without any cap.

But the saddest fact is that no employer can "win" a discrimination suit. Defending a litigation successfully still costs employers executive time and distraction and incurs considerable legal fees since the litigation most often requires the entire work records of both the terminee and the retained employees to be presented to the trier of fact.

### How to Keep a Firing from Backfiring

The best way to win litigation is to avoid it. So employers should plan litigation avoidance early and follow preventative human resource practices.

#### 1. The Time To Defend Begins Before Hire

The time to defend against termination lawsuits begins before an employee is hired. When employers hire someone, they enter into a contract of employment with that person. That contract may be oral (typically, what is discussed are wages, hours and benefits like medical insurance, holidays and vacations), but it is nevertheless binding on the employer.

If an employer wants to retain the prerogative of terminating an employee for any reason (other than those that are contrary to a statute or, in some states, to public policy), that had better be spelled out in writing and signed by the employee before or at hire. The best place is in a signed employment application spelling out at-will employment.

#### 2. Watch Out For Unintentional Promises

Great care should also be taken to review personnel manuals, employee bulletins and other documents that state terms of employment. High minded promises of fair treatment can result in lawsuits where juries decide what they think is fair.

#### 3. Cut Down Your Risks Before You Use The Ax

Be sure that there is a provable, unassailable business reason -- such as a clear violation of a published work rule or a documented record of warnings for poor performance or excessive absenteeism -- for any termination. That reason should be reviewed and established before the employee is let go, not after.

A typical recipe for a disastrous lawsuit involves a long term employee who received wage increases every year and whose personnel file contains no written warnings. One day someone decides that a formerly acceptable level of performance is inadequate. So the employee is unceremoniously let go. If the employee had been warned of substandard performance and given fair warning and a reasonable opportunity to improve, the employer would have a better case.

Another invitation to a lawsuit occurs when there are several employees with a chronic problem (like absenteeism), but the older employee is the first one fired. Better to discipline the worst first. When younger people, not in any protected group, with similar absenteeism problems are not terminated, the employer faces a strong inference that the real reason for termination was age. But if those with the worst absenteeism records are terminated first, especially after warnings, it will be harder to prove that hidden discrimination was the real reason.

### Ten Ways To Avoid (Or Win) Employment Termination Litigation

#### 1. SAY WHAT YOU MEAN -- YOU MAY BE STUCK WITH WHAT YOU SAY

Before hiring, review documents like employment applications and personnel manuals, that are likely to be involved in a termination lawsuit. Be sure that they promise only what you want them to deliver. Be sure that they spell out that oral promises will not change the written rules.

#### 2. LOOSE LIPS SINK SHIPS

Be sure no one in authority makes promises you do not intend to keep. And tell employees that only properly promulgated written policies will be honored.

#### 3. FAIR WARNING WINS LAWSUITS -- COMMUNICATE WORK RULES AND WARNINGS

Establish basic, written work rules and make clear that infractions can lead to discipline and discharge. Don't adopt overly specific rules. Use rules like honesty, courtesy, excessive absenteeism, sobriety and a duty to cooperate in Company investigations. Be sure every employee receives a copy and signs for it. Use (but don't promise) progressive discipline for lesser infractions -- that is, give an employee an opportunity to correct unacceptable behavior. This might include a written warning or two acknowledged by the employee.

### 4. DISCIPLINE THE WORST FIRST

If discipline is necessary, deal with the worst offenders first.

### 5. LOOK BEFORE YOU LOP

Get the employee's side of the story in front of witnesses and, if possible, in writing signed by the employee. Then, check it out before you act. It is best to recognize factual weaknesses in your case before it is too late. If you really don't want the employee on the premises during the investigation, suspend the employee during your investigation.

### 6. CONSISTENCY IS THE BEST PREVENTATIVE

Be consistent in discipline -- similar infractions should receive similar punishment.

### 7. FAIR TREATMENT WINS CASES

Review the employee's personnel file with an eye to fairness: Fair treatment as well as fair warning. Ask yourself how you would react if you were an impartial juror. For example, employees with longer seniority merit more opportunities to correct their actions than newly hired people.

### 8. BUY OUT THE BAD RISKS

If you must fire someone but think your termination rationale could be viewed as suspect, consider severance pay in exchange for a release from any claims that might arise from the termination. Not the severance pay or vacation pay that you give to anyone who is terminated, but additional compensation. To be valid, a release must be knowing, voluntary and for a valuable consideration, over and above otherwise mandated severance benefits.

Under the Age Discrimination in Employment Act, you have to give 21 to 45 days to consider the release and must explicitly advise the terminee to consult a lawyer. It is best to have your lawyer draft the release.

### 9. NEVER SPEAK ILL OF THE RECENTLY DEPARTED

Don't stand in the way of the terminated employee's future employment. An employee who has a new job is less likely to bring a lawsuit against a previous employer. Bad references can lead to expensive lawsuits. But good references are an admission that there was not cause to terminate. So, adopt a policy of simply confirming dates of employment.

## 10. CONSIDER ALTERNATIVES TO JURIES LIKE ARBITRATION

Wouldn't you prefer to have a business person decide rather than a jury of employees? Why not offer or require Commercial Rules Arbitration of employment termination disputes before a fair and partial arbitrator.

To these general rules add one more: Know which laws are applicable in your jurisdiction.

One way to avoid juries is to require employees to submit their claims through a grievance procedure internally and then to mediation (nonbinding) and or binding arbitration. While arbitration is easier for employees to use, experience has shown that a thoughtful grievance procedure diffuses heat which could lead to costly litigation.

-30-

# Appendix B: Relating the Internal Control Structure to Assertions

# Relating the Internal Control
## Structure to Assertions

| Relevant Internal Control Structure Policy or Procedure | Why Policy or Procedure is Relevant to Assertion |
|---|---|

### ACCOUNTS RECEIVABLE

- Credit manager approves credit for customer orders over $5,000.

  ➜ Reduce losses from uncollectible credit sales.

- Credit manager follows up on customer complaints on monthly statements.

  ➜ Identify erroneous amounts or transactions charged to customers.

- Quantities shipped are reconciled to quantities billed.

  ➜ Insure that all goods shipped are billed and all goods billed are shipped.

- Owner-manager reviews aged customer trial balance each quarter.

  ➜ Identify potential collection problems and review makeup of receivables.

- Approved price lists are used for billing.

  ➜ Ensure that customers are charged the correct price.

### REVENUE CYCLE

- Compare budgeted with actual sales and analyze significant variances.

  ➜ Significant variances of actual sales over budget may be due to recording sales that did not occur.

- Use prenumbered sales invoices and account for continuity of numerical sequence.*

  ➜ Using formal, controlled sales invoices as basis for recording sales helps insure that only sales transactions that actually occurred are recorded.

- Independently match sales invoices with evidence of shipment.*

  ➜ Ability to support sales invoice with evidence that goods were shipped helps substantiate that sale actually occurred before it is recorded.

- Mail monthly statements to customers.

  ➜ Customers are likely to report sales charged to their accounts that did not occur.

- Compare budgeted with actual sales and analyze significant variances.

  ➜ Significant variances of actual sales under budget may be due to failure to record sales.

- Use prenumbered shipping documents and account for continuity of numerical sequence.*

  ➜ Establishes a formal, controlled record that a shipment has occurred and should be recorded as a sales.

- Independently match shipping documents with sales invoices.*

  ➜ Ability to support shipping document with evidence that sale was invoiced helps substantiate that sale was recorded.

- Mail monthly statements to customers.

  ➜ Customers may report sales that have not been recorded in their accounts.

*Generally not a significant assertion for sales transactions*

- Use authorized price lists.

  ➜ Provides billing personnel with a predetermined approved price to charge customers.

-1-

| Relevant Internal Control Structure Policy or Procedure | Why Policy or Procedure is Relevant to Assertion |
|---|---|
| **SALES CONTROLS** | |
| • Independently review sales invoices for price list used and price charged. | ➔ Helps identify incorrect prices on invoices before billed to customers. |
| • Independently recompute sales invoice extensions and footings. | ➔ Helps identify incorrect extensions or footings on invoices before customer billed. |
| • Compare budgeted with actual sales and analyze significant variances. | ➔ Significant variances of actual sales over or under budget may be due to incorrect sales valuation. |
| • Mail monthly statements to customers. | ➔ Customers may report incorrect amounts charged to their accounts because of incorrect sales valuation. |
| • Conduct credit check or review payment performance to approve credit.* | ➔ Helps insure that customers can pay for credit sales and, thus, accounts receivable are properly valued. |
| • Use chart of accounts with adequate detail. | ➔ Helps identify specific accounts in which sales should be classified when recorded. |
| • Independently review account codings on sales documents. | ➔ Helps identify incorrect account classifications before sale recorded. |
| • Compare budgeted with actual sales and analyze significant variances. | ➔ Significant variances of actual sales over or under budget may be due to incorrect transaction classification. |
| • Mail monthly statements to customers. | ➔ Customers may report errors in their accounts caused by incorrect sales classification. |
| • Use disclosure checklists. | ➔ Helps insure that all necessary disclosures have been made and that adequate information has been disclosed. |
| • Independently review disclosures. | ➔ Helps insure that disclosures are complete and accurate. |
| **SALES ADJUSTMENTS** | |
| • Follow established policies for granting cash discounts, returns, and allowances; and for determining uncollectible accounts. | ➔ Helps insure that only legitimate sales adjustments are recorded. |
| • Use prenumbered sales adjustment forms, account for continuity of numerical sequence, and require approval for adjustment be recorded on form.* | ➔ Using formal, controlled sales adjustment forms as basis for recording sales adjustment transactions helps insure that only sales adjustments that actually occurred are recorded. |
| • Independently review sales adjustment approval. | ➔ Helps insure that a legitimate sales adjustment occurred. |
| • Use prenumbered sales adjustment forms and account for continuity of numerical sequence.* | ➔ Establishes a formal, controlled record that a sales adjustment has occurred and should be recorded. |
| • Mail monthly statements to customers. | ➔ Customers may report sales adjustments that have not |

-2-

| Relevant Internal Control Structure Policy or Procedure | Why Policy or Procedure is Relevant to Assertion |
|---|---|
| | been recorded in their accounts. |
| *Generally not a significant assertion for sales adjustment transactions* <br>• Mail monthly statements to customers. | ➔ Customers may report incorrect amounts recorded in their accounts because of incorrect sales adjustment valuation. |
| • Independently review sales adjustments. | ➔ May identify incorrect valuation of sales adjustments. |
| **COLLECTIONS** <br>• Use prenumbered remittance advices or prepare cash receipt lists. | ➔ Using formal controlled records as basis for recording cash collection transactions helps insure that only cash collections that occurred are recorded. |
| • Prepare monthly bank reconcilliations. | ➔ May identify cash collections recorded in the accounting records but not deposited in the bank because they did not actually occur. |
| • Store cash in secure locations. | ➔ Restricts access to cash on hand to authorized individuals and helps prevent misappropriation. |
| • Use prenumbered remittance advices or prepare cash receipt lists. | ➔ Establishes a formal, controlled record of cash collections received in the mail that should be recorded. |
| • Use cash registers for cash sales. | ➔ Establishes a formal controlled record of cash sales that should be recorded. |
| • Endorse checks restrictively. | ➔ Requires that checks be deposited only to company account, which helps insure they will be recorded in accounting records. |
| • Prepare monthly bank reconcilliations. | ➔ May identify cash collections deposited in bank but not recorded in the accounting records. |
| • Mail monthly statements to customers. | ➔ Customers may report cash paid to client but not recorded in their account. |
| • Compare budgeted with actual cash collections and analyze significant variances. | ➔ Significant variances of cash collections under budget may be due to failure to record cash collections. |
| **PURCHASING CONTROLS** <br>• Use prenumbered requisitions, purchase orders, and receiving reports, and account for their numerical sequence.* | ➔ Establishes formal, controlled records documenting that a purchase occurred. |
| • Independently review authorizations of purchase requisitions and purchase orders and independently match vendor invoice with those documents and with related receiving report.* | ➔ Ability to support vendor invoice with authorized requisition, order, and receiving report helps substantiate that a purchase occurred. |

-3-

| Relevant Internal Control Structure Policy or Procedure | Why Policy or Procedure is Relevant to Assertion |
|---|---|
| • Cancel purchase transaction documents immediately after processing. | ➔ Cancellation prevents documents from being reused to support another transaction. |
| • Reconcile vendors' statements with accounts payable records. | ➔ Accounts payable records may contain purchase transactions not on vendor statements because they did not occur. |
| • Compare budgeted with actual purchases and analyze significant variances. | ➔ Significant variances of actual purchases over budget may be due to recording purchases that did not occur. |
| • Use prenumbered purchase requisitions, purchase orders, and receiving reports, and account for their numerical sequences.* | ➔ Establishes formal, controlled records that an order and receipt have occurred and should be recorded as a purchase. |
| • Reconcile vendors' statements with accounts payable records. | ➔ Vendor statements may identify purchases that have not been recorded in accounts payable records but should be. |
| • Use checklists or budgets to determine whether all purchased services have been recorded. | ➔ Checklists and budget analysis help identify services received that should be recorded as purchases. |
| • Require that documentation for consignment orders and receipts clearly specifies a consignment transaction. | ➔ Helps prevent consignment transactions from being recorded as purchases. |
| • Require that goods received on consignment are tagged or physically separated from purchased goods. | ➔ Helps prevent consigned goods from being recorded as purchases. |
| • Independently compare item description, quantities, and prices on vendor invoices with related data on purchase requisitions, orders and receiving reports.* | ➔ Helps identify incorrect items, quantities, and prices on vendor invoices before recorded as purchases. |
| • Independently recompute extensions and footings on vendor invoices.* | ➔ Helps identify incorrect extensions or footings on vendor invoices before recorded as purchases. |
| • Reconcile vendors' statements with accounts payable records. | ➔ Incorrect valuation of purchases recorded in accounts payable may be identified by comparison with vendor statements. |
| • Compare budgeted with actual purchases and analyze significant variances. | ➔ Significant variances of actual purchases over or under budget may be due to incorrect purchases valuation. |
| • Use chart of accounts with adequate detail. | ➔ Helps identify specific accounts in which purchases should be classified when recorded. |
| • Independently review account codings on purchase requisitions, orders, or vendor invoices. | ➔ Helps identify incorrect account classifications before purchase recorded. |

| Relevant Internal Control Structure Policy or Procedure | Why Policy or Procedure is Relevant to Assertion |
|---|---|
| • Compare budgeted with actual purchases and analyze significant variances. | ➔ Significant variances of actual purchases over or under budget may be due to incorrect transaction classification. |
| • Use disclosure checklists. | ➔ Helps insure that all disclosures have been made and that adequate information has been disclosed. |
| • Independently review disclosures. | ➔ Helps insure that disclosures are complete and accurate. |

*CASH PAYMENT/ACCOUNTS PAYABLE*

| | |
|---|---|
| • Use prenumbered checks and account for continuity of numerical sequence.* | ➔ Establishes a formal, controlled record documenting that a cash payment occurred. |
| • Authorize specific individual(s) to sign checks. | ➔ Confines authority for issuing checks, thus reducing likelihood that invalid cash payments will be recorded. |
| • Prepare monthly bank reconciliation. | ➔ May identify cash payments recorded in the accounting records but not recorded in the bank statement because they did not occur. |
| • Use prenumbered checks and account for their numerical sequence.* | ➔ Establishes a formal, controlled record of cash payments made that should be recorded. |
| • Periodically compare issued checks with cash disbursements journal.* | ➔ May identify checks issued but not recorded in the accounting records. |
| • Prepare monthly bank reconciliation. | ➔ May identify cash payments recorded in the bank statement that were not recorded in the accounting records. |

*PAYROLL CONTROLS*

| | |
|---|---|
| • Use authorized hiring and termination documents and independently compare them with payroll.* | ➔ Establishing that legitimate employees exist helps substantiate that recorded payroll transactions actually occurred. |
| • Use time clocks and time cards, and require supervisory approval of time cards. | ➔ Using authorized record of time worked as basis for recording payroll transactions helps insure that only payroll transactions that actually occurred are recorded. |
| • Independently compare approved time cards with payroll.* | ➔ Independent verification of authorized record of time worked helps substantiate that recorded payroll transactions actually occurred. |
| • Analyze and follow up on labor variances. | ➔ Excess of actual over standard labor may be due to recording payroll transactions that did not occur. |
| • Segregate functions of personnel, timekeeping, and payroll disbursements. | ➔ Helps prevent recording payroll transactions for nonexistent employees. |

-5-

| Relevant Internal Control Structure<br>Policy or Procedure | Why Policy or Procedure is Relevant to<br>Assertion |
|---|---|
| • Use prenumbered payroll checks and account for their numerical sequence.* | ➜ Establishes formal, controlled record of payroll disbursements that should be recorded. |
| • Perform independent payroll bank reconciliation.* | ➜ May identify payroll disbursements recorded in payroll account bank statement that were not recorded in accounting records. |
| • Analyze and follow up on labor variances. | ➜ Excess of standard over actual labor may be due to payroll transactions that occurred but were not recorded. |
| • Segregate functions of payroll preparation, check signing and disbursement, and recording of payroll. | ➜ Segregation of these functions reduces opportunity to approve and make payroll disbursements and intentionally or unintentionally fail to record them. |

*Generally not a significant assertion for payroll transactions.*

| | |
|---|---|
| • Independently compare approved pay rates, deductions, and time cards with payroll computations.* | ➜ Helps insure that accurate pay rates, deductions, and time worked are used to make and record payroll computations. |
| • Independently recompute gross wages, deductions, and net pay. | ➜ May detect errors in payroll calculations prior to recording payroll. |
| • Analyze and follow up on labor variances. | ➜ Significant variances of actual and standard labor may be due to incorrect payroll valuation. |
| • Use chart of accounts with adequate detail. | ➜ Helps identify specific accounts in which payroll transactions should be classified when recorded. |
| • Independently review account codings for payroll transactions.* | ➜ Helps identify incorrect account classifications before payroll transactions are recorded. |
| • Analyze and follow up on labor variances. | ➜ Significant variances of actual and standard labor may be due to incorrect payroll classification. |

**PRODUCTION**

| | |
|---|---|
| • Use prenumbered and authorized requisitions, production orders, job cost sheets, and inspection reports and account for their numerical sequences.* | ➜ Using authorized, controlled production documents as basis for recording production transactions helps insure that only production transactions that actually occurred are recorded. |
| • Independently compare requisitions, production orders, job cost sheets and inspection reports for consistency.* | ➜ Ability to support production transaction with consistent production documents helps substantiate that transaction actually occurred before it is recorded. |
| • Reconcile production labor costs and overhead on job orders with payroll records and overhead incurred.* | ➜ Inability to reconcile labor or overhead costs charged to job orders with payroll or overhead records may be due to recording charges that did not occur. |
| • Analyze and follow up on materials and overhead variances. | ➜ Excess of actual over standard material, labor, or overhead cost may be due to recording transactions that |

-6-

| Relevant Internal Control Structure Policy or Procedure | Why Policy or Procedure is Relevant to Assertion |
|---|---|
| | did not occur. |
| • Reconcile goods placed in production, completed production, and finished goods additions.* | ➔ Inability to reconcile goods placed in production, completed or added with finished goods may be due to recording production transactions that did not occur. |
| • Use perpetual inventory records and periodically compare with physical inventory count. | ➔ Perpetual records document the occurrence of inventory transactions, and periodic comparisons with physical inventory may identify recorded inventory transactions that did not occur. |
| • Use secured inventory storage areas and security personnel and systems. | ➔ Helps insure that inventory exists by protecting against unintentional removal of inventory. |
| • Use prenumbered requisitions, production orders, job cost sheets, and inspection reports, and account for their numerical sequence.* | ➔ Using formal controlled records to document production transactions helps insure that production transactions will be recorded. |
| • Independently compare requisitions, production orders, job cost sheets, and inspection reports for consistency and reconciliation with accounting records.* | ➔ Comparison of production documents for consistency and tracing them to accounting records may identify unrecorded production transactions. |
| • Analyze and follow up on materials and overhead variances. | ➔ Excess of standard over actual material, labor or overhead cost may be due to failure to record production transactions. |
| • Reconcile goods placed in production, completed production, and finished goods additions.* | ➔ Inability to reconcile goods placed in production, completed, or added with finished goods may be due to failure to record production transactions. |
| • Use perpetual inventory records and periodically compare with physical inventory count. | ➔ Perpetual records document the recording of inventory transactions, and periodic comparisons with physical inventory may identify inventory transactions that should have been recorded but were not. |
| *Generally not a significant assertion for production transactions* <br> • Independently compare raw materials quantities and prices on requisitions, production orders, and job orders for consistency.* | ➔ Helps identify errors in recording quantities and prices on production documents as inventory moves through the production process. |
| • Independently compare raw materials prices on requisitions to vendor invoices or perpetual inventory records.* | ➔ Helps identify inaccurate raw material prices before they are used to value inventory. |

| Relevant Internal Control Structure Policy or Procedure | Why Policy or Procedure is Relevant to Assertion |
|---|---|
| • Independently review departmental overhead rates used on job orders and recompute overhead charged to jobs.* | ➜ Helps identify incorrect overhead rates or overhead computations on job orders before they are used to value inventory. |
| | ➜ Helps identify inaccurate extensions and footings in production documents before they are used to value inventory. |
| • Analyze and follow up on material, labor, and overhead variances. | ➜ Excess of standard over actual material, labor, or overhead costs may be due to incorrect valuation of materials, labor, or overhead. |
| • Use perpetual inventory records. | ➜ Provides a record of inventory usage and quantities on hand that helps prevent excess production or ordering of goods which results in slow-moving or obsolete inventory. |
| • Use sales forecasts or economic production run models. | ➜ Helps avoid production or ordering of excess goods which results in slow-moving or obsolete inventory. |
| • Establish effective product specifications and inspections. | ➜ Helps avoid production of defective or unsaleable goods and resulting overvaluation of inventory. |
| • Use chart of accounts with adequate detail. | ➜ Helps identify specific accounts in which production transactions should be classified when recorded. |
| • Independently review account codings for materials, labor, and overhead costs.* | ➜ Helps identify incorrect account classifications in materials, labor and overhead before production transactions are recorded. |
| • Reconcile production labor and overhead costs on job cost sheets with payroll and overhead accounting records.* | ➜ Inability to reconcile labor or overhead costs charged to job orders with payroll or overhead records may be due to misclassification of such costs. |
| • Use disclosure checklists. | ➜ Serves as a reminder of the disclosures that should be made and of the information the disclosures should contain. |
| • Independently review disclosures. | ➜ Helps identify incomplete or inaccurate disclosures. |

# Appendix C: New Metrics for a New Age

# New Metrics for a New Age

## Financial

- Total assets ($)
- Total assets/employee ($)
- Revenues/total assets (%)
- Profits/total assets (%)
- Revenues resulting from new business operations ($)
- Profits resulting from new business operations ($)
- Revenues/employee ($)
- Customer time/employee attendance (%)
- Profits/employee ($)
- Lost business revenues compared to market average (%)
- Revenues from new customers/total revenues (%)
- Market value ($)
- Return on net asset value (%)
- Return on net assets resulting from new business operations ($)
- Value added/employee ($)
- Value added/IT-employees ($)
- Investments in IT ($)

## Process

- Administrative expense/total revenues (%)
- Cost for administrative error/management revenues (%)
- Processing time, outpayments (#)
- Contracts filed without error (#)
- Function points/employee-month (#)
- PCs/employee (#)
- Laptops/employee (#)
- Administrative expense/employee ($)
- IT expense/employee ($)
- IT expense/administrative expense (%)
- Administrative expense/gross premium (%)
- IT capacity [CPU & DASD] (#)
- Change in IT inventory ($)
- Corporate quality goal (#)
- Corporate performance/quality goal (%)
- Discontinued IT inventory/IT inventory (%)
- Orphan IT inventory/IT inventory (%)
- IT capacity/employee (#)
- IT performance/employee (#)

-1-

## Customer

⇨ Market share (%)
⇨ Number of customers (#)
⇨ Annual sales/customer ($)
⇨ Customers lost (#)
⇨ Average duration of customer relationship (#)
⇨ Average customer size ($)
⇨ Customer rating (%)
⇨ Customer visits to the company (#)
⇨ Days visiting customers (#)
⇨ Customers/employee (#)
⇨ Field salespeople (#)
⇨ Field sales management (#)
⇨ Average time from customer contact to sales response (#)
⇨ Sales closed/sales contacts (%)
⇨ Satisfied customer index (%)
⇨ IT investment/salesperson ($)
⇨ IT investment/service & support employee ($)
⇨ Support expense/customer ($)
⇨ Service expense/customer/year ($)
⇨ Service expense/customer/contact ($)

## Human Resources

⇨ Leadership index (#)
⇨ Motivation index (#)
⇨ Empowerment index (#)
⇨ Number of employees (#)
⇨ Employee turnover (%)
⇨ Average employee years of service with company (#)
⇨ Number of managers (#)
⇨ Number of women managers (#)
⇨ Average age of employees (#)
⇨ Share of employees less than 40 years (%)
⇨ Time in training (days/year) (#)
⇨ Number of directors (#)
⇨ Number of women directors (#)
⇨ Number of full-time or permanent employees (#)
⇨ Average age of full-time or permanent employees (#)
⇨ Average years with company of full-time or permanent employees (#)
⇨ Annual turnover of full-time permanent employees (#)
⇨ Per capita annual cost of training, communication, and support programs for full-time permanent employees ($)
⇨ Full-time or permanent employees who spend less than 50% of work hours at a corporate facility (#)
⇨ Percentage of full-time permanent employees (%)
⇨ Per capita annual cost of training, communication, and support programs ($)
⇨ Number of full-time temporary employees (#)
⇨ Average years with company of full-time temporary employees (#)
⇨ Per capita annual cost of training and support programs for full-time temporary employees ($)
⇨ Number of part-time employees or non-full-time contractors (#), average duration of contract (#)
⇨ Company managers with advanced degrees: business (%), science and engineering (%), liberal arts (%)

## Renewal & Development

- Competence development expense/employee ($)
- Satisfied employee index (#)
- Marketing expense/customer ($)
- Share of training hours (%)
- Share of development hours (%)
- Employee's view (empowerment index) (#)
- R&D expense/administrative expense (%)
- Training expense/employee ($)
- Training expense/administrative expense (%)
- Business development expense/administrative expense (%)
- Share of employees below age 40 (%)
- IT development expense/IT expense (%)
- IT expenses on training/IT expense (%)
- R&D resources/total resources (%)
- Customer base (#)
- Average customer age (#)
- Average customer education (#)
- Average customer income ($)
- Average customer duration with company (months) (#)
- Training investment/customer ($)
- Direct communications to customer/year (#)
- Non-product-related expense/customer/year ($)
- New market development investment ($)
- Industry development investment ($)
- Value of EDI system ($)
- Upgrades to EDI system ($)
- Capacity of EDI system (#)
- Ratio of new products (less than 2 years old) to full company catalog (%)
- Ratio of new products (less than 2 years old) to product family (%)
- R&D invested in basic research (%)
- R&D invested in product design (%)
- R&D invested in processes (%)
- Investment in new product support and training ($)
- Average age of company patents (#)
- Patents pending (#)

-3-

# Afterword

We have tried, in this book, to address the issues that have come up again and again over the years as we have helped rapidly growing entrepreneurial companies to acquire the infrastructure they need to keep expanding and to fulfill their goals.

While each situation is unique, there seems to come a moment in nearly every expanding business when that business hits the wall —the point beyond which it cannot continue to grow without growing its own internal life-support systems.

We hope that this book will help entrepreneurial companies to recognize that moment—possibly even to anticipate that moment—and to take the steps necessary to get beyond.

As we've gone over the stories that make up this book, we've been filled with a renewed sense of admiration for the entrepreneurial spirit and energy that have driven these companies and the men and women who founded them. The individuals who have taken an idea and, through their own determination and drive, turned it into a company deserve our highest respect and admiration. If we have helped them to realize their goals, we can only say that it has been, and continues to be, our privilege.

# Index

**219**